Notes on Life

by

Joseph Conrad

The Echo Library 2008

Published by

The Echo Library

Echo Library
131 High St.
Teddington
Middlesex TW11 8HH

www.echo-library.com

Please report serious faults in the text to complaints@echo-library.com

ISBN 978-1-40689-033-4

NOTES ON LIFE & LETTERS

Contents:

Author's note

AUTHOR'S NOTE

I don't know whether I ought to offer an apology for this collection which has more to do with life than with letters. Its appeal is made to orderly minds. This, to be frank about it, is a process of tidying up, which, from the nature of things, cannot be regarded as premature. The fact is that I wanted to do it myself because of a feeling that had nothing to do with the considerations of worthiness or unworthiness of the small (but unbroken) pieces collected within the covers of this volume. Of course it may be said that I might have taken up a broom and used it without saying anything about it. That, certainly, is one way of tidying up.

But it would have been too much to have expected me to treat all this matter as removable rubbish. All those things had a place in my life. Whether any of them deserve to have been picked up and ranged on the shelf—this shelf—I cannot say, and, frankly, I have not allowed my mind to dwell on the question. I was afraid of thinking myself into a mood that would hurt my feelings; for those pieces of writing, whatever may be the comment on their display, appertain to the character of the man.

And so here they are, dusted, which was but a decent thing to do, but in no way polished, extending from the year '98 to the year '20, a thin array (for such a stretch of time) of really innocent attitudes: Conrad literary, Conrad political, Conrad reminiscent, Conrad controversial. Well, yes! A one-man show—or is it merely the show of one man?

The only thing that will not be found amongst those Figures and Things that have passed away, will be Conrad *en pantoufles*. It is a constitutional inability. *Schlafrock und pantoffeln*! Not that! Never! . . . I don't know whether I dare boast like a certain South American general who used to say that no emergency of war or peace had ever found him "with his boots off"; but I may say that whenever the various periodicals mentioned in this book called on me to come out and blow the trumpet of personal opinions or strike the pensive lute that speaks of the past, I always tried to pull on my boots first. I didn't want to do it, God knows! Their Editors, to whom I beg to offer my thanks here, made me perform mainly by kindness but partly by bribery. Well, yes! Bribery? What can you expect? I never pretended to be better than the people in the next street, or even in the same street.

This volume (including these embarrassed introductory remarks) is as near as I shall ever come to *deshabille* in public; and perhaps it will do something to help towards a better vision of the man, if it gives no more than a partial view of a piece of his back, a little dusty (after the process of tidying up), a little bowed, and receding from the world not because of weariness or misanthropy but for other reasons that cannot be helped: because the leaves fall, the water flows, the clock ticks with that horrid pitiless solemnity which you must have observed in the ticking of the hall clock at home. For reasons like that. Yes! It recedes. And this was the chance to afford one more view of it—even to my own eyes.

The section within this volume called Letters explains itself, though I do not pretend to say that it justifies its own existence. It claims nothing in its defence except the right of speech which I believe belongs to everybody outside a Trappist monastery. The part I have ventured, for shortness' sake, to call Life, may perhaps justify itself by the emotional sincerity of the feelings to which the various papers included under that head owe their origin. And as they relate to events of which everyone has a date, they are in the nature of sign-posts pointing out the direction my thoughts were compelled to take at the various cross-roads. If anybody detects any sort of consistency in the choice, this will be only proof positive that wisdom had nothing to do with it. Whether right or wrong, instinct alone is invariable; a fact which only adds a deeper shade to its inherent mystery. The appearance of intellectuality these pieces may present at first sight is merely the result of the arrangement of words. The logic that may be found there is only the logic of the language. But I need not labour the point. There will be plenty of people sagacious enough to perceive the absence of all wisdom from these pages. But I believe sufficiently in human sympathies to imagine that very few will question their sincerity. Whatever delusions I may have suffered from I have had no delusions as to the nature of the facts commented on here. I may have misjudged their import: but that is the sort of error for which one may expect a certain amount of toleration.

The only paper of this collection which has never been published before is the Note on the Polish Problem. It was written at the request of a friend to be shown privately, and its "Protectorate" idea, sprung from a strong sense of the critical nature of the situation, was shaped by the actual circumstances of the time. The time was about a month before the entrance of Roumania into the war, and though, honestly, I had seen already the shadow of coming events I could not permit my misgivings to enter into and destroy the structure of my plan. I still believe that there was some sense in it. It may certainly be charged with the appearance of lack of faith and it lays itself open to the throwing of many stones; but my object was practical and I had to consider warily the preconceived notions of the people to whom it was implicitly addressed, and also their unjustifiable hopes. They were unjustifiable, but who was to tell them that? I mean who was wise enough and convincing enough to show them the inanity of their mental attitude? The whole atmosphere was poisoned with visions that were not so much false as simply impossible. They were also the result of vague and unconfessed fears, and that made their strength. For myself, with a very definite dread in my heart, I was careful not to allude to their character because I did not want the Note to be thrown away unread. And then I had to remember that the impossible has sometimes the trick of coming to pass to the confusion of minds and often to the crushing of hearts.

Of the other papers I have nothing special to say. They are what they are, and I am by now too hardened a sinner to feel ashamed of insignificant indiscretions. And as to their appearance in this form I claim that indulgence to which all sinners against themselves are entitled.

J. C.   1920.

PART I—LETTERS

BOOKS—1905.

I.

"I have not read this author's books, and if I have read them I have forgotten what they were about."

These words are reported as having been uttered in our midst not a hundred years ago, publicly, from the seat of justice, by a civic magistrate. The words of our municipal rulers have a solemnity and importance far above the words of other mortals, because our municipal rulers more than any other variety of our governors and masters represent the average wisdom, temperament, sense and virtue of the community. This generalisation, it ought to be promptly said in the interests of eternal justice (and recent friendship), does not apply to the United States of America. There, if one may believe the long and helpless indignations of their daily and weekly Press, the majority of municipal rulers appear to be thieves of a particularly irrepressible sort. But this by the way. My concern is with a statement issuing from the average temperament and the average wisdom of a great and wealthy community, and uttered by a civic magistrate obviously without fear and without reproach.

I confess I am pleased with his temper, which is that of prudence. "I have not read the books," he says, and immediately he adds, "and if I have read them I have forgotten." This is excellent caution. And I like his style: it is unartificial and bears the stamp of manly sincerity. As a reported piece of prose this declaration is easy to read and not difficult to believe. Many books have not been read; still more have been forgotten. As a piece of civic oratory this declaration is strikingly effective. Calculated to fall in with the bent of the popular mind, so familiar with all forms of forgetfulness, it has also the power to stir up a subtle emotion while it starts a train of thought—and what greater force can be expected from human speech? But it is in naturalness that this declaration is perfectly delightful, for there is nothing more natural than for a grave City Father to forget what the books he has read once—long ago—in his giddy youth maybe—were about.

And the books in question are novels, or, at any rate, were written as novels. I proceed thus cautiously (following my illustrious example) because being without fear and desiring to remain as far as possible without reproach, I confess at once that I have not read them.

I have not; and of the million persons or more who are said to have read them, I never met one yet with the talent of lucid exposition sufficiently developed to give me a connected account of what they are about. But they are books, part and parcel of humanity, and as such, in their ever increasing, jostling multitude, they are worthy of regard, admiration, and compassion.

Especially of compassion. It has been said a long time ago that books have their fate. They have, and it is very much like the destiny of man. They share with us the great incertitude of ignominy or glory—of severe justice and senseless persecution—of calumny and misunderstanding—the shame of undeserved success. Of all the inanimate objects, of all men's creations, books are the nearest to us, for they contain our very thought, our ambitions, our indignations, our illusions, our fidelity to truth, and our persistent leaning towards error. But most of all they resemble us in their precarious hold on life. A bridge constructed according to the rules of the art of bridge-building is certain of a long, honourable and useful career. But a book as good in its way as the bridge may perish obscurely on the very day of its birth. The art of their creators is not sufficient to give them more than a moment of life. Of the books born from the restlessness, the inspiration, and the vanity of human minds, those that the Muses would love best lie more than all others under the menace of an early death. Sometimes their defects will save them. Sometimes a book fair to see may—to use a lofty expression—have no individual soul. Obviously a book of that sort cannot die. It can only crumble into dust. But the best of books drawing sustenance from the sympathy and memory of men have lived on the brink of destruction, for men's memories are short, and their sympathy is, we must admit, a very fluctuating, unprincipled emotion.

No secret of eternal life for our books can be found amongst the formulas of art, any more than for our bodies in a prescribed combination of drugs. This is not because some books are not worthy of enduring life, but because the formulas of art are dependent on things variable, unstable and untrustworthy; on human sympathies, on prejudices, on likes and dislikes, on the sense of virtue and the sense of propriety, on beliefs and theories that, indestructible in themselves, always change their form—often in the lifetime of one fleeting generation.

II.

Of all books, novels, which the Muses should love, make a serious claim on our compassion. The art of the novelist is simple. At the same time it is the most elusive of all creative arts, the most liable to be obscured by the scruples of its servants and votaries, the one pre-eminently destined to bring trouble to the mind and the heart of the artist. After all, the creation of a world is not a small undertaking except perhaps to the divinely gifted. In truth every novelist must begin by creating for himself a world, great or little, in which he can honestly believe. This world cannot be made otherwise than in his own image: it is fated to remain individual and a little mysterious, and yet it must resemble something already familiar to the experience, the thoughts and the sensations of his readers. At the heart of fiction, even the least worthy of the name, some sort of truth can be found—if only the truth of a childish theatrical ardour in the game of life, as in the novels of Dumas the father. But the fair truth of human delicacy can be found in Mr. Henry James's novels; and the comical, appalling truth of human rapacity let loose amongst the spoils of existence lives in the monstrous world created by Balzac. The pursuit of happiness by means lawful and unlawful, through resignation or revolt, by the clever manipulation of conventions or by solemn hanging on to the skirts of the latest scientific theory, is the only theme that can be legitimately developed by the novelist who is the chronicler of the adventures of mankind amongst the dangers of the kingdom of the earth. And the kingdom of this earth itself, the ground upon which his individualities stand, stumble, or die, must enter into his scheme of faithful record. To encompass all this in one harmonious conception is a great feat; and even to attempt it deliberately with serious intention, not from the senseless prompting of an ignorant heart, is an honourable ambition. For it requires some courage to step in calmly where fools may be eager to rush. As a distinguished and successful French novelist once observed of fiction, "C'est un art *trop* difficile."

It is natural that the novelist should doubt his ability to cope with his task. He imagines it more gigantic than it is. And yet literary creation being only one of the legitimate forms of human activity has no value but on the condition of not excluding the fullest recognition of all the more distinct forms of action. This condition is sometimes forgotten by the man of letters, who often, especially in his youth, is inclined to lay a claim of exclusive superiority for his own amongst all the other tasks of the human mind. The mass of verse and prose may glimmer here and there with the glow of a divine spark, but in the sum of human effort it has no special importance. There is no justificative formula for its existence any more than for any other artistic achievement. With the rest of them it is destined to be forgotten, without, perhaps, leaving the faintest trace. Where a novelist has an advantage over the workers in other fields of thought is in his privilege of freedom—the freedom of expression and the freedom of confessing his innermost beliefs—which should console him for the hard slavery of the pen.

III.

Liberty of imagination should be the most precious possession of a novelist. To try voluntarily to discover the fettering dogmas of some romantic, realistic, or naturalistic creed in the free work of its own inspiration, is a trick worthy of human perverseness which, after inventing an absurdity, endeavours to find for it a pedigree of distinguished ancestors. It is a weakness of inferior minds when it is not the cunning device of those who, uncertain of their talent, would seek to add lustre to it by the authority of a school. Such, for instance, are the high priests who have proclaimed Stendhal for a prophet of Naturalism. But Stendhal himself would have accepted no limitation of his freedom. Stendhal's mind was of the first order. His spirit above must be raging with a peculiarly Stendhalesque scorn and indignation. For the truth is that more than one kind of intellectual cowardice hides behind the literary formulas. And Stendhal was pre-eminently courageous. He wrote his two great novels, which so few people have read, in a spirit of fearless liberty.

It must not be supposed that I claim for the artist in fiction the freedom of moral Nihilism. I would require from him many acts of faith of which the first would be the cherishing of an undying hope; and hope, it will not be contested, implies all the piety of effort and renunciation. It is the God-sent form of trust in the magic force and inspiration belonging to the life of this earth. We are inclined to forget that the way of excellence is in the intellectual, as distinguished from emotional, humility. What one feels so hopelessly barren in declared pessimism is just its arrogance. It seems as if the discovery made by many men at various times that there is much evil in the world were a source of proud and unholy joy unto some of the modern writers. That frame of mind is not the proper one in which to approach seriously the art of fiction. It gives an author— goodness only knows why—an elated sense of his own superiority. And there is nothing more dangerous than such an elation to that absolute loyalty towards his feelings and sensations an author should keep hold of in his most exalted moments of creation.

To be hopeful in an artistic sense it is not necessary to think that the world is good. It is enough to believe that there is no impossibility of its being made so. If the flight of imaginative thought may be allowed to rise superior to many moralities current amongst mankind, a novelist who would think himself of a superior essence to other men would miss the first condition of his calling. To have the gift of words is no such great matter. A man furnished with a long-range weapon does not become a hunter or a warrior by the mere possession of a fire-arm; many other qualities of character and temperament are necessary to make him either one or the other. Of him from whose armoury of phrases one in a hundred thousand may perhaps hit the far-distant and elusive mark of art I would ask that in his dealings with mankind he should be capable of giving a tender recognition to their obscure virtues. I would not have him impatient with their small failings and scornful of their errors. I would not have him expect too much gratitude from that humanity whose fate, as illustrated in individuals, it is open to him to depict as ridiculous or terrible. I would wish him to look with a large forgiveness at men's ideas and prejudices, which are by no means the outcome of malevolence, but depend on their education, their social status, even their professions. The good artist should expect no recognition of his toil and no admiration of his genius, because his toil can with difficulty be appraised and his genius cannot possibly mean anything to the illiterate who, even from the dreadful wisdom of their evoked dead, have, so far, culled nothing but inanities and platitudes. I would wish him to enlarge his sympathies by patient and loving observation while he grows in mental power. It is in the impartial practice of life, if anywhere, that the promise of perfection for his art can be found, rather than in the absurd formulas trying to prescribe this or that particular method of technique or conception. Let him mature the strength of his imagination amongst the things of this earth, which it is his business to cherish and know, and refrain from calling down his inspiration ready-made from some heaven of perfections of which he knows nothing. And I would not grudge him the proud illusion that will come sometimes to a writer: the illusion that his achievement has almost equalled the greatness of his dream. For what else could give him the serenity and the force to hug to his breast as a thing delightful and human, the virtue, the rectitude and sagacity of his own City, declaring with simple eloquence through the mouth of a Conscript Father: "I have not read this author's books, and if I have read them I have forgotten . . ."

HENRY JAMES—AN APPRECIATION—1905

The critical faculty hesitates before the magnitude of Mr. Henry James's work. His books stand on my shelves in a place whose accessibility proclaims the habit of frequent communion. But not all his books. There is no collected edition to date, such as some of "our masters" have been provided with; no neat rows of volumes in buckram or half calf, putting forth a hasty claim to completeness, and conveying to my mind a hint of finality, of a surrender to fate of that field in which all these victories have been won. Nothing of the sort has been done for Mr. Henry James's victories in England.

In a world such as ours, so painful with all sorts of wonders, one would not exhaust oneself in barren marvelling over mere bindings, had not the fact, or rather the absence of the material fact, prominent in the case of other men whose writing counts, (for good or evil)—had it not been, I say, expressive of a direct truth spiritual and intellectual; an accident of—I suppose—the publishing business acquiring a symbolic meaning from its negative nature. Because, emphatically, in the body of Mr. Henry James's work there is no suggestion of finality, nowhere a hint of surrender, or even of probability of surrender, to his own victorious achievement in that field where he is a master. Happily, he will never be able to claim completeness; and, were he to confess to it in a moment of self-ignorance, he would not be believed by the very minds for whom such a confession naturally would be meant. It is impossible to think of Mr. Henry James becoming "complete" otherwise than by the brutality of our common fate whose finality is meaningless—in the sense of its logic being of a material order, the logic of a falling stone.

I do not know into what brand of ink Mr. Henry James dips his pen; indeed, I heard that of late he had been dictating; but I know that his mind is steeped in the waters flowing from the fountain of intellectual youth. The thing—a privilege—a miracle—what you will—is not quite hidden from the meanest of us who run as we read. To those who have the grace to stay their feet it is manifest. After some twenty years of attentive acquaintance with Mr. Henry James's work, it grows into absolute conviction which, all personal feeling apart, brings a sense of happiness into one's artistic existence. If gratitude, as someone defined it, is a lively sense of favours to come, it becomes very easy to be grateful to the author of The Ambassadors—to name the latest of his works. The favours are sure to come; the spring of that benevolence will never run dry. The stream of inspiration flows brimful in a predetermined direction, unaffected by the periods of drought, untroubled in its clearness by the storms of the land of letters, without languor or violence in its force, never running back upon itself, opening new visions at every turn of its course through that richly inhabited country its fertility has created for our delectation, for our judgment, for our exploring. It is, in fact, a magic spring.

With this phrase the metaphor of the perennial spring, of the inextinguishable youth, of running waters, as applied to Mr. Henry James's inspiration, may be dropped. In its volume and force the body of his work may be compared rather to a majestic river. All creative art is magic, is evocation of the unseen in forms persuasive, enlightening, familiar and surprising, for the edification of mankind, pinned down by the conditions of its existence to the earnest consideration of the most insignificant tides of reality.

Action in its essence, the creative art of a writer of fiction may be compared to rescue work carried out in darkness against cross gusts of wind swaying the action of a great multitude. It is rescue work, this snatching of vanishing phases of turbulence, disguised in fair words, out of the native obscurity into a light where the struggling forms may be seen, seized upon, endowed with the only possible form of permanence in this world of relative values—the permanence of memory. And the multitude feels it obscurely too; since the demand of the individual to the artist is, in effect, the cry, "Take me out of myself!" meaning really, out of my perishable activity into the light of imperishable consciousness. But everything is relative, and the light of consciousness is only enduring, merely the most enduring of the things of this earth, imperishable only as against the short-lived work of our industrious hands.

When the last aqueduct shall have crumbled to pieces, the last airship fallen to the ground, the last blade of grass have died upon a dying earth, man, indomitable by his training in resistance to misery and pain, shall set this undiminished light of his eyes against the feeble glow of the sun. The artistic faculty, of which each of us has a minute grain, may find its voice in some individual of that last group, gifted with a power of expression and courageous enough to interpret the ultimate experience of mankind in terms of his temperament, in terms of art. I do not mean to say that he would attempt to beguile the last moments of humanity by an ingenious tale. It would be too much to expect—from humanity. I doubt the heroism of the hearers. As to the heroism of the artist, no doubt is necessary. There would be on his part no heroism. The artist in his calling of interpreter creates (the clearest form of demonstration) because he must. He is so much of a voice that, for him, silence is like death; and the postulate was, that there is a group alive, clustered on his threshold to watch the last flicker of light on a black sky, to hear the last word uttered in the stilled workshop of the earth. It is safe to affirm that, if anybody, it will be the imaginative man who would be moved to speak on the eve of that day without to-morrow—whether in austere exhortation or in a phrase of sardonic comment, who can guess?

For my own part, from a short and cursory acquaintance with my kind, I am inclined to think that the last utterance will formulate, strange as it may appear, some hope now to us utterly inconceivable. For mankind is delightful in its pride, its assurance, and its indomitable tenacity. It will sleep on the battlefield among its own dead, in the manner of an army having won a barren victory. It will not know when it is beaten. And perhaps it is right in that quality. The victories are not, perhaps, so barren as it may appear from a purely strategical, utilitarian point of view. Mr. Henry James seems to hold that belief. Nobody has rendered better, perhaps, the tenacity of temper, or known how to drape the robe of spiritual honour about the drooping form of a victor in a barren strife.

And the honour is always well won; for the struggles Mr. Henry James chronicles with such subtle and direct insight are, though only personal contests, desperate in their silence, none the less heroic (in the modern sense) for the absence of shouted watchwords, clash of arms and sound of trumpets. Those are adventures in which only choice souls are ever involved. And Mr. Henry James records them with a fearless and insistent fidelity to the *peripeties* of the contest, and the feelings of the combatants.

The fiercest excitements of a romance *de cape et d'epee*, the romance of yard-arm and boarding pike so dear to youth, whose knowledge of action (as of other things) is imperfect and limited, are matched, for the quickening of our maturer years, by the tasks set, by the difficulties presented, to the sense of truth, of necessity—before all, of conduct—of Mr. Henry James's men and women. His mankind is delightful. It is delightful in its tenacity; it refuses to own itself beaten; it will sleep on the battlefield. These warlike images come by themselves under the pen; since from the duality of man's nature and the competition of individuals, the life-history of the earth must in the last instance be a history of a really very relentless warfare. Neither his fellows, nor his gods, nor his passions will leave a man alone. In virtue of these allies and enemies, he holds his precarious dominion, he possesses his fleeting significance; and it is this relation in all its manifestations, great and little, superficial or profound, and this relation alone, that is commented upon, interpreted, demonstrated by the art of the novelist in the only possible way in which the task can be performed: by the independent creation of circumstance and character, achieved against all the difficulties of expression, in an imaginative effort finding its inspiration from the reality of forms and sensations. That a sacrifice must be made, that something has to be given up, is the truth engraved in the innermost recesses of the fair temple built for our edification by the masters of fiction. There is no other secret behind the curtain. All adventure, all love, every success is resumed in the supreme energy of an act of renunciation. It is the uttermost limit of our power; it is the most potent and effective force at our disposal on which rest the labours of a solitary man in his study, the rock on which have been built commonwealths whose might casts a dwarfing shadow upon two oceans. Like a natural force which is obscured as much as illuminated by the multiplicity of phenomena, the power of renunciation is obscured by the mass of weaknesses, vacillations, secondary motives and false steps and compromises which make up the sum of our activity. But no man or woman worthy of the name can pretend to anything more, to anything greater. And Mr. Henry James's men and women are worthy of the name, within the limits his art, so clear, so sure of itself, has drawn round their activities. He would be the last to claim for them Titanic proportions. The earth itself has grown smaller in the course of ages. But in every sphere of human perplexities and emotions, there are more greatnesses than one—not counting here the greatness of the artist himself. Wherever he stands, at the beginning or the end of things, a man has to sacrifice his gods to his passions, or his passions to his gods. That is the problem, great enough, in all truth, if approached in the spirit of sincerity and knowledge.

In one of his critical studies, published some fifteen years ago, Mr. Henry James claims for the novelist the standing of the historian as the only adequate one, as for himself and before his audience. I think that the claim cannot be contested, and that the position is unassailable. Fiction is history, human history, or it is nothing. But it is also more than that; it stands on firmer ground, being based on the reality of forms and the observation of social phenomena, whereas history is based on documents, and the reading of print and handwriting—on second-hand impression. Thus fiction is nearer truth. But let that pass. A historian may be an artist too, and a novelist is a historian, the preserver, the keeper, the expounder, of human experience. As is meet for a man of his descent and tradition, Mr. Henry James is the historian of fine consciences.

Of course, this is a general statement; but I don't think its truth will be, or can be questioned. Its fault is that it leaves so much out; and, besides, Mr. Henry James is much too considerable to be put into the nutshell of a phrase. The fact remains that he has made his choice, and that his choice is justified up to the hilt by the success of his art. He has taken for himself the greater part. The range of a fine conscience covers more good and evil than the range of conscience which may be called, roughly, not fine; a conscience, less troubled by the nice discrimination of shades of conduct. A fine conscience is more concerned with essentials; its triumphs are more perfect, if less profitable, in a worldly sense. There is, in short, more truth in its working for a historian to detect and to show. It is a thing of infinite complication and suggestion. None of these escapes the art of Mr. Henry James. He has mastered the country, his domain, not wild indeed, but full of romantic glimpses, of deep shadows and sunny places. There are no secrets left within his range. He has disclosed them as they should be disclosed—that is, beautifully. And, indeed, ugliness has but little place in this world of his creation. Yet, it is always felt in the truthfulness of his art; it is there, it surrounds the scene, it presses close upon it. It is made visible, tangible, in the struggles, in the contacts of the fine consciences, in their perplexities, in the sophism of their mistakes. For a fine conscience is naturally a virtuous one. What is natural about it is just its fineness, an abiding sense of the intangible, ever-present, right. It is most visible in their ultimate triumph, in their emergence from miracle, through an energetic act of renunciation. Energetic, not violent: the distinction is wide, enormous, like that between substance and shadow.

Through it all Mr. Henry James keeps a firm hold of the substance, of what is worth having, of what is worth holding. The contrary opinion has been, if not absolutely affirmed, then at least implied, with some frequency. To most of us, living willingly in a sort of intellectual moonlight, in the faintly reflected light of truth, the shadows so firmly renounced by Mr. Henry James's men and women, stand out endowed with extraordinary value, with a value so extraordinary that their rejection offends, by its uncalled-for scrupulousness, those business-like instincts which a careful Providence has implanted in our breasts. And, apart from that just cause of discontent, it is obvious that a solution by rejection must always present a certain lack of finality, especially startling when contrasted with the usual methods of solution by rewards and punishments, by crowned love, by fortune, by a broken leg or a sudden death. Why the reading public which, as a body, has never laid upon a story-teller the command to be an artist, should demand from him this sham of Divine Omnipotence, is utterly incomprehensible. But so it is; and these solutions are legitimate inasmuch as they satisfy the desire for finality, for which our hearts yearn with a longing greater than the longing for the loaves and fishes of this earth. Perhaps the only true desire of mankind, coming thus to light in its hours of leisure, is to be set at rest. One is never set at rest by Mr. Henry James's novels. His books end as an episode in life ends. You remain with the sense of the life still going on; and even the subtle presence of the dead is felt in that silence that comes upon the artist-creation when the last word has been read. It is eminently satisfying, but it is not final. Mr. Henry James, great artist and faithful historian, never attempts the impossible.

ALPHONSE DAUDET—1898

It is sweet to talk decorously of the dead who are part of our past, our indisputable possession. One must admit regretfully that to-day is but a scramble, that to-morrow may never come; it is only the precious yesterday that cannot be taken away from us. A gift from the dead, great and little, it makes life supportable, it almost makes one believe in a benevolent scheme of creation. And some kind of belief is very necessary. But the real knowledge of matters infinitely more profound than any conceivable scheme of creation is with the dead alone. That is why our talk about them should be as decorous as their silence. Their generosity and their discretion deserve nothing less at our hands; and they, who belong already to the unchangeable, would probably disdain to claim more than this from a mankind that changes its loves and its hates about every twenty-five years—at the coming of every new and wiser generation.

One of the most generous of the dead is Daudet, who, with a prodigality approaching magnificence, gave himself up to us without reserve in his work, with all his qualities and all his faults. Neither his qualities nor his faults were great, though they were by no means imperceptible. It is only his generosity that is out of the common. What strikes one most in his work is the disinterestedness of the toiler. With more talent than many bigger men, he did not preach about himself, he did not attempt to persuade mankind into a belief of his own greatness. He never posed as a scientist or as a seer, not even as a prophet; and he neglected his interests to the point of never propounding a theory for the purpose of giving a tremendous significance to his art, alone of all things, in a world that, by some strange oversight, has not been supplied with an obvious meaning. Neither did he affect a passive attitude before the spectacle of life, an attitude which in gods—and in a rare mortal here and there—may appear godlike, but assumed by some men, causes one, very unwillingly, to think of the melancholy quietude of an ape. He was not the wearisome expounder of this or that theory, here to-day and spurned to-morrow. He was not a great artist, he was not an artist at all, if you like—but he was Alphonse Daudet, a man as naively clear, honest, and vibrating as the sunshine of his native land; that regrettably undiscriminating sunshine which matures grapes and pumpkins alike, and cannot, of course, obtain the commendation of the very select who look at life from under a parasol.

Naturally, being a man from the South, he had a rather outspoken belief in himself, but his small distinction, worth many a greater, was in not being in bondage to some vanishing creed. He was a worker who could not compel the admiration of the few, but who deserved the affection of the many; and he may be spoken of with tenderness and regret, for he is not immortal—he is only dead. During his life the simple man whose business it ought to have been to climb, in the name of Art, some elevation or other, was content to remain below, on the plain, amongst his creations, and take an eager part in those disasters, weaknesses, and joys which are tragic enough in their droll way, but are by no means so momentous and profound as some writers—probably for the sake of Art—would like to make us believe. There is, when one thinks of it, a considerable want of candour in the august view of life. Without doubt a cautious reticence on the subject, or even a delicately false suggestion thrown out in that direction is, in a way, praiseworthy, since it helps to uphold the dignity of man—a matter of great importance, as anyone can see; still one cannot help feeling that a certain amount of sincerity would not be wholly blamable. To state, then, with studied moderation a belief that in unfortunate moments of lucidity is irresistibly borne in upon most of us—the blind agitation caused mostly by hunger and complicated by love and ferocity does not deserve either by its beauty, or its morality, or its possible results, the artistic fuss made over it. It may be consoling—for human folly is very *bizarre*—but it is scarcely honest to shout at those who struggle drowning in an insignificant pool: You are indeed admirable and great to be the victims of such a profound, of such a terrible ocean!

And Daudet was honest; perhaps because he knew no better—but he was very honest. If he saw only the surface of things it is for the reason that most things have nothing but a surface. He did not pretend—perhaps because he did not know how—he did not pretend to see any depths in a life that is only a film of unsteady appearances stretched over regions deep indeed, but which have nothing to do with the half-truths, half-thoughts, and whole illusions of existence. The road to these distant regions does not lie through the domain of Art or the domain of Science where well-known voices quarrel noisily in a misty emptiness; it is a path of toilsome silence upon which travel men simple and unknown, with closed lips, or, maybe, whispering their pain softly—only to themselves.

But Daudet did not whisper; he spoke loudly, with animation, with a clear felicity of tone—as a bird sings. He saw life around him with extreme clearness, and he felt it as it is—thinner than air and more elusive than a flash of lightning. He hastened to offer it his compassion, his indignation, his wonder, his sympathy, without giving a moment of thought to the momentous issues that are supposed to lurk in the logic of such sentiments. He tolerated the little foibles, the small ruffianisms, the grave mistakes; the only thing he distinctly would not forgive was hardness of heart. This unpractical attitude would have been fatal to a better man, but his readers have forgiven him. Withal he is chivalrous to exiled queens and deformed sempstresses, he is pityingly tender to broken-down actors, to ruined gentlemen, to stupid Academicians; he is glad of the joys of the commonplace people in a commonplace way—and he never makes a secret of all this. No, the man was not an artist. What if his creations are illumined by the sunshine of his temperament so vividly that they stand before us infinitely more real than the dingy illusions surrounding our everyday existence? The misguided man is for ever pottering amongst them, lifting up his voice, dotting his i's in the wrong places. He takes Tartarin by the arm, he does not conceal his interest in the Nabob's cheques, his sympathy for an honest Academician *plus bête que nature*, his hate for an architect *plus mauvais que la gale*; he is in the thick of it all. He feels with the Duc de Mora and with Felicia Ruys—

and he lets you see it. He does not sit on a pedestal in the hieratic and imbecile pose of some cheap god whose greatness consists in being too stupid to care. He cares immensely for his Nabobs, his kings, his book-keepers, his Colettes, and his Saphos. He vibrates together with his universe, and with lamentable simplicity follows M. de Montpavon on that last walk along the Boulevards.

"Monsieur de Montpavon marche a la mort," and the creator of that unlucky *gentilhomme* follows with stealthy footsteps, with wide eyes, with an impressively pointing finger. And who wouldn't look? But it is hard; it is sometimes very hard to forgive him the dotted i's, the pointing finger, this making plain of obvious mysteries. "Monsieur de Montpavon marche a la mort," and presently, on the crowded pavement, takes off his hat with punctilious courtesy to the doctor's wife, who, elegant and unhappy, is bound on the same pilgrimage. This is too much! We feel we cannot forgive him such meetings, the constant whisper of his presence. We feel we cannot, till suddenly the very *naivete* of it all touches us with the revealed suggestion of a truth. Then we see that the man is not false; all this is done in transparent good faith. The man is not melodramatic; he is only picturesque. He may not be an artist, but he comes as near the truth as some of the greatest. His creations are seen; you can look into their very eyes, and these are as thoughtless as the eyes of any wise generation that has in its hands the fame of writers. Yes, they are *seen*, and the man who is not an artist is seen also commiserating, indignant, joyous, human and alive in their very midst. Inevitably they *marchent a la mort*—and they are very near the truth of our common destiny: their fate is poignant, it is intensely interesting, and of not the slightest consequence.

GUY DE MAUPASSANT—1904[1]

To introduce Maupassant to English readers with apologetic explanations as though his art were recondite and the tendency of his work immoral would be a gratuitous impertinence.

Maupassant's conception of his art is such as one would expect from a practical and resolute mind; but in the consummate simplicity of his technique it ceases to be perceptible. This is one of its greatest qualities, and like all the great virtues it is based primarily on self- denial.

To pronounce a judgment upon the general tendency of an author is a difficult task. One could not depend upon reason alone, nor yet trust solely to one's emotions. Used together, they would in many cases traverse each other, because emotions have their own unanswerable logic. Our capacity for emotion is limited, and the field of our intelligence is restricted. Responsiveness to every feeling, combined with the penetration of every intellectual subterfuge, would end, not in judgment, but in universal absolution. *Tout comprendre c'est tout pardonner.* And in this benevolent neutrality towards the warring errors of human nature all light would go out from art and from life.

We are at liberty then to quarrel with Maupassant's attitude towards our world in which, like the rest of us, he has that share which his senses are able to give him. But we need not quarrel with him violently. If our feelings (which are tender) happen to be hurt because his talent is not exercised for the praise and consolation of mankind, our intelligence (which is great) should let us see that he is a very splendid sinner, like all those who in this valley of compromises err by over-devotion to the truth that is in them. His determinism, barren of praise, blame and consolation, has all the merit of his conscientious art. The worth of every conviction consists precisely in the steadfastness with which it is held.

Except for his philosophy, which in the case of so consummate an artist does not matter (unless to the solemn and naive mind), Maupassant of all writers of fiction demands least forgiveness from his readers. He does not require forgiveness because he is never dull.

The interest of a reader in a work of imagination is either ethical or that of simple curiosity. Both are perfectly legitimate, since there is both a moral and an excitement to be found in a faithful rendering of life. And in Maupassant's work there is the interest of curiosity and the moral of a point of view consistently preserved and never obtruded for the end of personal gratification. The spectacle of this immense talent served by exceptional faculties and triumphing over the most thankless subjects by an unswerving singleness of purpose is in itself an admirable lesson in the power of artistic honesty, one may say of artistic virtue. The inherent greatness of the man consists in this, that he will let none of the fascinations that beset a writer working in loneliness turn him away from the straight path, from the vouchsafed vision of excellence. He will not be led into perdition by the seductions of sentiment, of eloquence, of humour, of pathos; of

---

[1] Yvette and Other Stories. Translated by Ada Galsworthy.

all that splendid pageant of faults that pass between the writer and his probity on the blank sheet of paper, like the glittering cortege of deadly sins before the austere anchorite in the desert air of Thebaide. This is not to say that Maupassant's austerity has never faltered; but the fact remains that no tempting demon has ever succeeded in hurling him down from his high, if narrow, pedestal.

It is the austerity of his talent, of course, that is in question. Let the discriminating reader, who at times may well spare a moment or two to the consideration and enjoyment of artistic excellence, be asked to reflect a little upon the texture of two stories included in this volume: "A Piece of String," and "A Sale." How many openings the last offers for the gratuitous display of the author's wit or clever buffoonery, the first for an unmeasured display of sentiment! And both sentiment and buffoonery could have been made very good too, in a way accessible to the meanest intelligence, at the cost of truth and honesty. Here it is where Maupassant's austerity comes in. He refrains from setting his cleverness against the eloquence of the facts. There is humour and pathos in these stories; but such is the greatness of his talent, the refinement of his artistic conscience, that all his high qualities appear inherent in the very things of which he speaks, as if they had been altogether independent of his presentation. Facts, and again facts are his unique concern. That is why he is not always properly understood. His facts are so perfectly rendered that, like the actualities of life itself, they demand from the reader the faculty of observation which is rare, the power of appreciation which is generally wanting in most of us who are guided mainly by empty phrases requiring no effort, demanding from us no qualities except a vague susceptibility to emotion. Nobody has ever gained the vast applause of a crowd by the simple and clear exposition of vital facts. Words alone strung upon a convention have fascinated us as worthless glass beads strung on a thread have charmed at all times our brothers the unsophisticated savages of the islands. Now, Maupassant, of whom it has been said that he is the master of the *mot juste*, has never been a dealer in words. His wares have been, not glass beads, but polished gems; not the most rare and precious, perhaps, but of the very first water of their kind.

That he took trouble with his gems, taking them up in the rough and polishing each facet patiently, the publication of the two posthumous volumes of short stories proves abundantly. I think it proves also the assertion made here that he was by no means a dealer in words. On looking at the first feeble drafts from which so many perfect stories have been fashioned, one discovers that what has been matured, improved, brought to perfection by unwearied endeavour is not the diction of the tale, but the vision of its true shape and detail. Those first attempts are not faltering or uncertain in expression. It is the conception which is at fault. The subjects have not yet been adequately seen. His proceeding was not to group expressive words, that mean nothing, around misty and mysterious shapes dear to muddled intellects and belonging neither to earth nor to heaven. His vision by a more scrupulous, prolonged and devoted attention to the aspects of the visible world discovered at last the right words as if miraculously impressed for him upon the face of things and events. This was the particular shape taken by his inspiration; it came to him directly, honestly in the light of his day, not on the tortuous, dark roads of meditation. His realities came to him from a genuine source, from this universe of vain appearances wherein we men have found everything to make us proud, sorry, exalted, and humble.

Maupassant's renown is universal, but his popularity is restricted. It is not difficult to perceive why. Maupassant is an intensely national writer. He is so intensely national in his logic, in his clearness, in his aesthetic and moral conceptions, that he has been accepted by his countrymen without having had to pay the tribute of flattery either to the nation as a whole, or to any class, sphere or division of the nation. The truth of his art tells with an irresistible force; and he stands excused from the duty of patriotic posturing. He is a Frenchman of Frenchmen beyond question or cavil, and with that he is simple enough to be universally comprehensible. What is wanting to his universal success is the mediocrity of an obvious and appealing tenderness. He neglects to qualify his truth with the drop of facile sweetness; he forgets to strew paper roses over the tombs. The disregard of these common decencies lays him open to the charges of cruelty, cynicism, hardness. And yet it can be safely affirmed that this man wrote from the fulness of a compassionate heart. He is merciless and yet gentle with his mankind; he does not rail at their prudent fears and their small artifices; he does not despise their labours. It seems to me that he looks with an eye of profound pity upon their troubles, deceptions and misery. But he looks at them all. He sees—and does not turn away his head. As a matter of fact he is courageous.

Courage and justice are not popular virtues. The practice of strict justice is shocking to the multitude who always (perhaps from an obscure sense of guilt) attach to it the meaning of mercy. In the majority of us, who want to be left alone with our illusions, courage inspires a vague alarm. This is what is felt about Maupassant. His qualities, to use the charming and popular phrase, are not lovable. Courage being a force will not masquerade in the robes of affected delicacy and restraint. But if his courage is not of a chivalrous stamp, it cannot be denied that it is never brutal for the sake of effect. The writer of these few reflections, inspired by a long and intimate acquaintance with the work of the man, has been struck by the appreciation of Maupassant manifested by many women gifted with tenderness and intelligence. Their more delicate and audacious souls are good judges of courage. Their finer penetration has discovered his genuine masculinity without display, his virility without a pose. They have discerned in his faithful dealings with the world that enterprising and fearless temperament, poor in ideas but rich in power, which appeals most to the feminine mind.

It cannot be denied that he thinks very little. In him extreme energy of perception achieves great results, as in men of action the energy of force and desire. His view of intellectual problems is perhaps more simple than their nature warrants; still a man who has written *Yvette* cannot be accused of want of subtlety. But one cannot insist enough upon this, that his subtlety, his humour, his grimness, though no doubt they are his own, are never presented otherwise but as belonging to our life, as found in nature, whose beauties and cruelties alike breathe the spirit of serene unconsciousness.

Maupassant's philosophy of life is more temperamental than rational. He expects nothing from gods or men. He trusts his senses for information and his instinct for deductions. It may seem that he has made but little use of his mind. But let me be clearly understood. His sensibility is really very great; and it is impossible to be sensible, unless one thinks vividly, unless one thinks correctly, starting from intelligible premises to an unsophisticated conclusion.

This is literary honesty. It may be remarked that it does not differ very greatly from the ideal honesty of the respectable majority, from the honesty of law-givers, of warriors, of kings, of bricklayers, of all those who express their fundamental sentiment in the ordinary course of their activities, by the work of their hands.

The work of Maupassant's hands is honest. He thinks sufficiently to concrete his fearless conclusions in illuminative instances. He renders them with that exact knowledge of the means and that absolute devotion to the aim of creating a true effect—which is art. He is the most accomplished of narrators.

It is evident that Maupassant looked upon his mankind in another spirit than those writers who make haste to submerge the difficulties of our holding-place in the universe under a flood of false and sentimental assumptions. Maupassant was a true and dutiful lover of our earth. He says himself in one of his descriptive passages: "Nous autres que seduit la terre . . ." It was true. The earth had for him a compelling charm. He looks upon her august and furrowed face with the fierce insight of real passion. His is the power of detecting the one immutable quality that matters in the changing aspects of nature and under the ever-shifting surface of life. To say that he could not embrace in his glance all its magnificence and all its misery is only to say that he was human. He lays claim to nothing that his matchless vision has not made his own. This creative artist has the true imagination; he never condescends to invent anything; he sets up no empty pretences. And he stoops to no littleness in his art—least of all to the miserable vanity of a catching phrase.

ANATOLE FRANCE—1904

I.—"CRAINQUEBILLE"

The latest volume of M. Anatole France purports, by the declaration of its title-page, to contain several profitable narratives. The story of Crainquebille's encounter with human justice stands at the head of them; a tale of a well-bestowed charity closes the book with the touch of playful irony characteristic of the writer on whom the most distinguished amongst his literary countrymen have conferred the rank of Prince of Prose.

Never has a dignity been better borne. M. Anatole France is a good prince. He knows nothing of tyranny but much of compassion. The detachment of his mind from common errors and current superstitions befits the exalted rank he holds in the Commonwealth of Literature. It is just to suppose that the clamour of the tribes in the forum had little to do with his elevation. Their elect are of another stamp. They are such as their need of precipitate action requires. He is the Elect of the Senate—the Senate of Letters—whose Conscript Fathers have recognised him as *primus inter pares*; a post of pure honour and of no privilege.

It is a good choice. First, because it is just, and next, because it is safe. The dignity will suffer no diminution in M. Anatole France's hands. He is worthy of a great tradition, learned in the lessons of the past, concerned with the present, and as earnest as to the future as a good prince should be in his public action. It is a Republican dignity. And M. Anatole France, with his sceptical insight into an forms of government, is a good Republican. He is indulgent to the weaknesses of the people, and perceives that political institutions, whether contrived by the wisdom of the few or the ignorance of the many, are incapable of securing the happiness of mankind. He perceives this truth in the serenity of his soul and in the elevation of his mind. He expresses his convictions with measure, restraint and harmony, which are indeed princely qualities. He is a great analyst of illusions. He searches and probes their innermost recesses as if they were realities made of an eternal substance. And therein consists his humanity; this is the expression of his profound and unalterable compassion. He will flatter no tribe no section in the forum or in the market-place. His lucid thought is not beguiled into false pity or into the common weakness of affection. He feels that men born in ignorance as in the house of an enemy, and condemned to struggle with error and passions through endless centuries, should be spared the supreme cruelty of a hope for ever deferred. He knows that our best hopes are irrealisable; that it is the almost incredible misfortune of mankind, but also its highest privilege, to aspire towards the impossible; that men have never failed to defeat their highest aims by the very strength of their humanity which can conceive the most gigantic tasks but leaves them disarmed before their irremediable littleness. He knows this well because he is an artist and a master; but he knows, too, that only in the continuity of effort there is a refuge from despair for minds less clear-seeing and philosophic than his own. Therefore he wishes us to believe and to hope, preserving in our activity the consoling illusion of power and intelligent purpose. He is a good and politic prince.

"The majesty of justice is contained entire in each sentence pronounced by the judge in the name of the sovereign people. Jerome Crainquebille, hawker of vegetables, became aware of the august aspect of the law as he stood indicted before the tribunal of the higher Police Court on a charge of insulting a constable of the force." With this exposition begins the first tale of M. Anatole France's latest volume.

The bust of the Republic and the image of the Crucified Christ appear side by side above the bench occupied by the President Bourriche and his two Assessors; all the laws divine and human are suspended over the head of Crainquebille.

From the first visual impression of the accused and of the court the author passes by a characteristic and natural turn to the historical and moral significance of those two emblems of State and Religion whose accord is only possible to the confused reasoning of an average man. But the reasoning of M. Anatole France is never confused. His reasoning is clear and informed by a profound erudition. Such is not the case of Crainquebille, a street hawker, charged with insulting the constituted power of society in the person of a policeman. The charge is not true, nothing was further from his thoughts; but, amazed by the novelty of his position, he does not reflect that the Cross on the wall perpetuates the memory of a sentence which for nineteen hundred years all the Christian peoples have looked upon as a grave miscarriage of justice. He might well have challenged the President to pronounce any sort of sentence, if it were merely to forty-eight hours of simple imprisonment, in the name of the Crucified Redeemer.

He might have done so. But Crainquebille, who has lived pushing every day for half a century his hand-barrow loaded with vegetables through the streets of Paris, has not a philosophic mind. Truth to say he has nothing. He is one of the disinherited. Properly speaking, he has no existence at all, or, to be strictly truthful, he had no existence till M. Anatole France's philosophic mind and human sympathy have called him up from his nothingness for our pleasure, and, as the title-page of the book has it, no doubt for our profit also.

Therefore we behold him in the dock, a stranger to all historical, political or social considerations which can be brought to bear upon his case. He remains lost in astonishment. Penetrated with respect, overwhelmed with awe, he is ready to trust the judge upon the question of his transgression. In his conscience he does not think himself culpable; but M. Anatole France's philosophical mind discovers for us that he feels all the insignificance of such a thing as the conscience of a mere street- hawker in the face of the symbols of the law and before the ministers of social repression. Crainquebille is innocent; but already the young advocate, his defender, has half persuaded him of his guilt.

On this phrase practically ends the introductory chapter of the story which, as the author's dedication states, has inspired an admirable draughtsman and a skilful dramatist, each in his art, to a vision of tragic grandeur. And this opening chapter without a name—consisting of two and a half pages, some four hundred words at most—is a masterpiece of insight and simplicity, resumed in M. Anatole France's distinction of thought and in his princely command of words.

It is followed by six more short chapters, concise and full, delicate and complete like the petals of a flower, presenting to us the Adventure of Crainquebille—Crainquebille before the justice—An Apology for the President of the Tribunal—Of the Submission of Crainquebille to the Laws of the Republic—Of his Attitude before the Public Opinion, and so on to the chapter of the Last Consequences. We see, created for us in his outward form and innermost perplexity, the old man degraded from his high estate of a law-abiding street-hawker and driven to insult, really this time, the majesty of the social order in the person of another police- constable. It is not an act of revolt, and still less of revenge. Crainquebille is too old, too resigned, too weary, too guileless to raise the black standard of insurrection. He is cold and homeless and starving. He remembers the warmth and the food of the prison. He perceives the means to get back there. Since he has been locked up, he argues with himself, for uttering words which, as a matter of fact he did not say, he will go forth now, and to the first policeman he meets will say those very words in order to be imprisoned again. Thus reasons Crainquebille with simplicity and confidence. He accepts facts. Nothing surprises him. But all the phenomena of social organisation and of his own life remain for him mysterious to the end. The description of the policeman in his short cape and hood, who stands quite still, under the light of a street lamp at the edge of the pavement shining with the wet of a rainy autumn evening along the whole extent of a long and deserted thoroughfare, is a perfect piece of imaginative precision. From under the edge of the hood his eyes look upon Crainquebille, who has just uttered in an uncertain voice the sacramental, insulting phrase of the popular slang—*Mort aux vaches*! They look upon him shining in the deep shadow of the hood with an expression of sadness, vigilance, and contempt.

He does not move. Crainquebille, in a feeble and hesitating voice, repeats once more the insulting words. But this policeman is full of philosophic superiority, disdain, and indulgence. He refuses to take in charge the old and miserable vagabond who stands before him shivering and ragged in the drizzle. And the ruined Crainquebille, victim of a ridiculous miscarriage of justice, appalled at this magnanimity, passes on hopelessly down the street full of shadows where the lamps gleam each in a ruddy halo of falling mist.

M. Anatole France can speak for the people. This prince of the Senate is invested with the tribunitian power. M. Anatole France is something of a Socialist; and in that respect he seems to depart from his sceptical philosophy. But as an illustrious statesman, now no more, a great prince too, with an ironic mind and a literary gift, has sarcastically remarked in one of his public speeches: "We are all Socialists now." And in the sense in which it may be said that we all in Europe are Christians that is true enough. To many of us Socialism is merely an emotion. An emotion is much and is also less than nothing. It is the initial impulse. The real Socialism of to-day is a religion. It has its dogmas. The value of the dogma does not consist in its truthfulness, and M. Anatole France, who loves truth, does not love dogma. Only, unlike religion, the cohesive strength of Socialism lies not in its dogmas but in its ideal. It is perhaps a too materialistic ideal, and the mind of M. Anatole France may not find in it either comfort or consolation. It is not to be doubted that he suspects this himself; but there is something reposeful in the finality of popular conceptions. M. Anatole France, a good prince and a good Republican, will succeed no doubt in being a good Socialist. He will disregard the stupidity of the dogma and the unlovely form of the ideal. His art will find its own beauty in the imaginative presentation of wrongs, of errors, and miseries that call aloud for redress. M. Anatole France is humane. He is also human. He may be able to discard his philosophy; to forget that the evils are many and the remedies are few, that there is no universal panacea, that fatality is invincible, that there is an implacable menace of death in the triumph of the humanitarian idea. He may forget all that because love is stronger than truth.

Besides "Crainquebille" this volume contains sixteen other stories and sketches. To define them it is enough to say that they are written in M. Anatole France's prose. One sketch entitled "Riquet" may be found incorporated in the volume of *Monsieur Bergeret a Paris*. "Putois" is a remarkable little tale, significant, humorous, amusing, and symbolic. It concerns the career of a man born in the utterance of a hasty and untruthful excuse made by a lady at a loss how to decline without offence a very pressing invitation to dinner from a very tyrannical aunt. This happens in a provincial town, and the lady says in effect: "Impossible, my dear aunt. To-morrow I am expecting the gardener." And the garden she glances at is a poor garden; it is a wild garden; its extent is insignificant and its neglect seems beyond remedy. "A gardener! What for?" asks the aunt. "To work in the garden." And the poor lady is abashed at the transparence of her evasion. But the lie is told, it is believed, and she sticks to it. When the masterful old aunt inquires, "What is the man's name, my dear?" she answers brazenly, "His name is Putois." "Where does he live?" "Oh, I don't know; anywhere. He won't give his address. One leaves a message for him here and there." "Oh! I see," says the other; "he is a sort of ne'er do well, an idler, a vagabond. I advise you, my dear, to be careful how you let such a creature into your grounds; but I have a large garden, and when you do not want his services I shall find him some work to do, and see he does it too. Tell your Putois to come and see me." And thereupon Putois is born; he stalks abroad, invisible, upon his career of vagabondage and crime, stealing melons from gardens and tea-spoons from pantries, indulging his licentious proclivities; becoming the talk of the town and of the countryside; seen simultaneously in far-distant places; pursued by gendarmes, whose brigadier assures the uneasy householders that he "knows that scamp very well, and won't be long in laying his hands upon him." A detailed description of his person collected from the information furnished by various people appears in the columns of a local newspaper. Putois lives in his strength and malevolence. He lives after the manner of legendary heroes, of the gods of Olympus. He is the creation of the popular mind. There comes a time when even the innocent originator of that mysterious and potent evil-doer is induced to believe for a moment that he may have a real and tangible presence. All this is told with the wit and the art and the philosophy which is familiar to

M. Anatole France's readers and admirers. For it is difficult to read M. Anatole France without admiring him. He has the princely gift of arousing a spontaneous loyalty, but with this difference, that the consent of our reason has its place by the side of our enthusiasm. He is an artist. As an artist he awakens emotion. The quality of his art remains, as an inspiration, fascinating and inscrutable; but the proceedings of his thought compel our intellectual admiration.

In this volume the trifle called "The Military Manoeuvres at Montil," apart from its far-reaching irony, embodies incidentally the very spirit of automobilism. Somehow or other, how you cannot tell, the flight over the country in a motor-car, its sensations, its fatigue, its vast topographical range, its incidents down to the bursting of a tyre, are brought home to you with all the force of high imaginative perception. It would be out of place to analyse here the means by which the true impression is conveyed so that the absurd rushing about of General Decuir, in a 30-horse-power car, in search of his cavalry brigade, becomes to you a more real experience than any day-and-night run you may ever have taken yourself. Suffice it to say that M. Anatole France had thought the thing worth doing and that it becomes, in virtue of his art, a distinct achievement. And there are other sketches in this book, more or less slight, but all worthy of regard—the childhood's recollections of Professor Bergeret and his sister Zoe; the dialogue of the two upright judges and the conversation of their horses; the dream of M. Jean Marteau, aimless, extravagant, apocalyptic, and of all the dreams one ever dreamt, the most essentially dreamlike. The vision of M. Anatole France, the Prince of Prose, ranges over all the extent of his realm, indulgent and penetrating, disillusioned and curious, finding treasures of truth and beauty concealed from less gifted magicians. Contemplating the exactness of his images and the justice of his judgment, the freedom of his fancy and the fidelity of his purpose, one becomes aware of the futility of literary watchwords and the vanity of all the schools of fiction. Not that M. Anatole France is a wild and untrammelled genius. He is not that. Issued legitimately from the past, he is mindful of his high descent. He has a critical temperament joined to creative power. He surveys his vast domain in a spirit of princely moderation that knows nothing of excesses but much of restraint.

II.—"L'ILE DES PINGOUINS"

M. Anatole France, historian and adventurer, has given us many profitable histories of saints and sinners, of Roman procurators and of officials of the Third Republic, of *grandes dames* and of dames not so very grand, of ornate Latinists and of inarticulate street hawkers, of priests and generals—in fact, the history of all humanity as it appears to his penetrating eye, serving a mind marvellously incisive in its scepticism, and a heart that, of all contemporary hearts gifted with a voice, contains the greatest treasure of charitable irony. As to M. Anatole France's adventures, these are well-known. They lie open to this prodigal world in the four volumes of the *Vie Litteraire*, describing the adventures of a choice soul amongst masterpieces. For such is the romantic view M. Anatole France takes of the life of a literary critic. History and adventure, then, seem to be the chosen fields for the magnificent evolutions of M. Anatole

France's prose; but no material limits can stand in the way of a **genius**. The latest book from his pen—which may be called golden, as the lips of **an eloquent** saint once upon a time were acclaimed golden by the faithful—this **latest** book is, up to a certain point, a book of travel.

I would not mislead a public whose confidence I court. The book is not a record of globe-trotting. I regret it. It would have been a joy to watch M. Anatole France pouring the clear elixir compounded of his Pyrrhonic philosophy, his Benedictine erudition, his gentle wit and most humane irony into such an unpromising and opaque vessel. He would have attempted it in a spirit of benevolence towards his fellow men and of compassion for that life of the earth which is but a vain and transitory illusion. M. Anatole France is a great magician, yet there seem to be tasks which he dare not face. For he is also a sage.

It is a book of ocean travel—not, however, as understood by Herr Ballin of Hamburg, the Machiavel of the Atlantic. It is a book of exploration and discovery—not, however, as conceived by an enterprising journal and a shrewdly philanthropic king of the nineteenth century. It is nothing so recent as that. It dates much further back; long, long before the dark age when Krupp of Essen wrought at his steel plates and a German Emperor condescendingly suggested the last improvements in ships' dining- tables. The best idea of the inconceivable antiquity of that enterprise I can give you is by stating the nature of the explorer's ship. It was a trough of stone, a vessel of hollowed granite.

The explorer was St. Mael, a saint of Armorica. I had never heard of him before, but I believe now in his arduous existence with a faith which is a tribute to M. Anatole France's pious earnestness and delicate irony. St. Mael existed. It is distinctly stated of him that his life was a progress in virtue. Thus it seems that there may be saints that are not progressively virtuous. St. Mael was not of that kind. He was industrious. He evangelised the heathen. He erected two hundred and eighteen chapels and seventy-four abbeys. Indefatigable navigator of the faith, he drifted casually in the miraculous trough of stone from coast to coast and from island to island along the northern seas. At the age of eighty-four his high stature was bowed by his long labours, but his sinewy arms preserved their vigour and his rude eloquence had lost nothing of its force.

A nautical devil tempting him by the worldly suggestion of fitting out his desultory, miraculous trough with mast, sail, and rudder for swifter progression (the idea of haste has sprung from the pride of Satan), the simple old saint lent his ear to the subtle arguments of the progressive enemy of mankind.

The venerable St. Mael fell away from grace by not perceiving at once that a gift of heaven cannot be improved by the contrivances of human ingenuity. His punishment was adequate. A terrific tempest snatched the rigged ship of stone in its whirlwinds, and, to be brief, the dazed St. Mael was stranded violently on the Island of Penguins.

The saint wandered away from the shore. It was a flat, round island whence rose in the centre a conical mountain capped with clouds. The rain was falling incessantly—a gentle, soft rain which caused the simple saint to exclaim in great delight: "This is the island of tears, the island of contrition!"

Meantime the inhabitants had flocked in their tens of thousands to an amphitheatre of rocks; they were penguins; but the holy man, rendered deaf and purblind by his years, mistook excusably the multitude of silly, erect, and self-important birds for a human crowd. At once he began to preach to them the doctrine of salvation. Having finished his discourse he lost no time in administering to his interesting congregation the sacrament of baptism.

If you are at all a theologian you will see that it was no mean adventure to happen to a well-meaning and zealous saint. Pray reflect on the magnitude of the issues! It is easy to believe what M. Anatole France says, that, when the baptism of the Penguins became known in Paradise, it caused there neither joy nor sorrow, but a profound sensation.

M. Anatole France is no mean theologian himself. He reports with great casuistical erudition the debates in the saintly council assembled in Heaven for the consideration of an event so disturbing to the economy of religious mysteries. Ultimately the baptised Penguins had to be turned into human beings; and together with the privilege of sublime hopes these innocent birds received the curse of original sin, with the labours, the miseries, the passions, and the weaknesses attached to the fallen condition of humanity.

At this point M. Anatole France is again an historian. From being the Hakluyt of a saintly adventurer he turns (but more concisely) into the Gibbon of Imperial Penguins. Tracing the development of their civilisation, the absurdity of their desires, the pathos of their folly and the ridiculous littleness of their quarrels, his golden pen lightens by relevant but unpuritanical anecdotes the austerity of a work devoted to a subject so grave as the Polity of Penguins. It is a very admirable treatment, and I hasten to congratulate all men of receptive mind on the feast of wisdom which is theirs for the mere plucking of a book from a shelf.

TURGENEV[2]—1917

Dear Edward,

I am glad to hear that you are about to publish a study of Turgenev, that fortunate artist who has found so much in life for us and no doubt for himself, with the exception of bare justice. Perhaps that will come to him, too, in time. Your study may help the consummation. For his luck persists after his death. What greater luck an artist like Turgenev could wish for than to find in the English-speaking world a translator who has missed none of the most delicate, most simple beauties of his work, and a critic who has known how to analyse and point out its high qualities with perfect sympathy and insight.

After twenty odd years of friendship (and my first literary friendship too) I may well permit myself to make that statement, while thinking of your wonderful Prefaces as they appeared from time to time in the volumes of Turgenev's complete edition, the last of which came into the light of public indifference in the ninety-ninth year of the nineteenth century.

With that year one may say, with some justice, that the age of Turgenev had come to an end too; yet work so simple and human, so independent of the transitory formulas and theories of art, belongs as you point out in the Preface to *Smoke* "to all time."

Turgenev's creative activity covers about thirty years. Since it came to an end the social and political events in Russia have moved at an accelerated pace, but the deep origins of them, in the moral and intellectual unrest of the souls, are recorded in the whole body of his work with the unerring lucidity of a great national writer. The first stirrings, the first gleams of the great forces can be seen almost in every page of the novels, of the short stories and of *A Sportsman's Sketches*—those marvellous landscapes peopled by unforgettable figures.

Those will never grow old. Fashions in monsters do change, but the truth of humanity goes on for ever, unchangeable and inexhaustible in the variety of its disclosures. Whether Turgenev's art, which has captured it with such mastery and such gentleness, is for "all time" it is hard to say. Since, as you say yourself, he brings all his problems and characters to the test of love, we may hope that it will endure at least till the infinite emotions of love are replaced by the exact simplicity of perfected Eugenics. But even by then, I think, women would not have changed much; and the women of Turgenev who understood them so tenderly, so reverently and so passionately—they, at least, are certainly for all time.

Women are, one may say, the foundation of his art. They are Russian of course. Never was a writer so profoundly, so whole-souledly national. But for non-Russian readers, Turgenev's Russia is but a canvas on which the incomparable artist of humanity lays his colours and his forms in the great light and the free air of the world. Had he invented them all and also every stick and stone, brook and hill and field in which they move, his personages would have

---

[2] *Turgenev.* A Study. By Edward Garnett.

been just as true and as poignant in their perplexed lives. They are his own and also universal. Any one can accept them with no more question than one accepts the Italians of Shakespeare.

In the larger, non-Russian view, what should make Turgenev sympathetic and welcome to the English-speaking world, is his essential humanity. All his creations, fortunate and unfortunate, oppressed and oppressors, are human beings, not strange beasts in a menagerie or damned souls knocking themselves to pieces in the stuffy darkness of mystical contradictions. They are human beings, fit to live, fit to suffer, fit to struggle, fit to win, fit to lose, in the endless and inspiring game of pursuing from day to day the ever-receding future.

I began by calling him lucky, and he was, in a sense. But one ends by having some doubts. To be so great without the slightest parade and so fine without any tricks of "cleverness" must be fatal to any man's influence with his contemporaries.

Frankly, I don't want to appear as qualified to judge of things Russian. It wouldn't be true. I know nothing of them. But I am aware of a few general truths, such as, for instance, that no man, whatever may be the loftiness of his character, the purity of his motives and the peace of his conscience—no man, I say, likes to be beaten with sticks during the greater part of his existence. From what one knows of his history it appears clearly that in Russia almost any stick was good enough to beat Turgenev with in his latter years. When he died the characteristically chicken-hearted Autocracy hastened to stuff his mortal envelope into the tomb it refused to honour, while the sensitive Revolutionists went on for a time flinging after his shade those jeers and curses from which that impartial lover of *all* his countrymen had suffered so much in his lifetime. For he, too, was sensitive. Every page of his writing bears its testimony to the fatal absence of callousness in the man.

And now he suffers a little from other things. In truth it is not the convulsed terror-haunted Dostoievski but the serene Turgenev who is under a curse. For only think! Every gift has been heaped on his cradle: absolute sanity and the deepest sensibility, the clearest vision and the quickest responsiveness, penetrating insight and unfailing generosity of judgment, an exquisite perception of the visible world and an unerring instinct for the significant, for the essential in the life of men and women, the clearest mind, the warmest heart, the largest sympathy—and all that in perfect measure. There's enough there to ruin the prospects of any writer. For you know very well, my dear Edward, that if you had Antinous himself in a booth of the world's fair, and killed yourself in protesting that his soul was as perfect as his body, you wouldn't get one per cent. of the crowd struggling next door for a sight of the Double- headed Nightingale or of some weak-kneed giant grinning through a horse collar.

J. C.

STEPHEN CRANE—A NOTE WITHOUT DATES—1919

My acquaintance with Stephen Crane was brought about by Mr. Pawling, partner in the publishing firm of Mr. William Heinemann.

One day Mr. Pawling said to me: "Stephen Crane has arrived in England. I asked him if there was anybody he wanted to meet and he mentioned two names. One of them was yours." I had then just been reading, like the rest of the world, Crane's *Red Badge of Courage*. The subject of that story was war, from the point of view of an individual soldier's emotions. That individual (he remains nameless throughout) was interesting enough in himself, but on turning over the pages of that little book which had for the moment secured such a noisy recognition I had been even more interested in the personality of the writer. The picture of a simple and untried youth becoming through the needs of his country part of a great fighting machine was presented with an earnestness of purpose, a sense of tragic issues, and an imaginative force of expression which struck me as quite uncommon and altogether worthy of admiration.

Apparently Stephen Crane had received a favourable impression from the reading of the *Nigger of the Narcissus*, a book of mine which had also been published lately. I was truly pleased to hear this.

On my next visit to town we met at a lunch. I saw a young man of medium stature and slender build, with very steady, penetrating blue eyes, the eyes of a being who not only sees visions but can brood over them to some purpose.

He had indeed a wonderful power of vision, which he applied to the things of this earth and of our mortal humanity with a penetrating force that seemed to reach, within life's appearances and forms, the very spirit of life's truth. His ignorance of the world at large—he had seen very little of it—did not stand in the way of his imaginative grasp of facts, events, and picturesque men.

His manner was very quiet, his personality at first sight interesting, and he talked slowly with an intonation which on some people, mainly Americans, had, I believe, a jarring effect. But not on me. Whatever he said had a personal note, and he expressed himself with a graphic simplicity which was extremely engaging. He knew little of literature, either of his own country or of any other, but he was himself a wonderful artist in words whenever he took a pen into his hand. Then his gift came out—and it was seen then to be much more than mere felicity of language. His impressionism of phrase went really deeper than the surface. In his writing he was very sure of his effects. I don't think he was ever in doubt about what he could do. Yet it often seemed to me that he was but half aware of the exceptional quality of his achievement.

This achievement was curtailed by his early death. It was a great loss to his friends, but perhaps not so much to literature. I think that he had given his measure fully in the few books he had the time to write. Let me not be misunderstood: the loss was great, but it was the loss of the delight his art could give, not the loss of any further possible revelation. As to himself, who can say how much he gained or lost by quitting so early this world of the living, which he knew how to set before us in the terms of his own artistic vision? Perhaps he did not lose a great deal. The recognition he was accorded was rather languid and given him grudgingly. The worthiest welcome he secured for his tales in this country was from Mr. W. Henley in the *New Review* and later, towards the end of his life, from the late Mr. William Blackwood in his magazine. For the rest I must say that during his sojourn in England he had the misfortune to be, as the French say, *mal entoure*. He was beset by people who understood not the quality of his genius and were antagonistic to the deeper fineness of his nature. Some of them have died since, but dead or alive they are not worth speaking about now. I don't think he had any illusions about them himself: yet there was a strain of good-nature and perhaps of weakness in his character which prevented him from shaking himself free from their worthless and patronising attentions, which in those days caused me much secret irritation whenever I stayed with him in either of his English homes. My wife and I like best to remember him riding to meet us at the gate of the Park at Brede. Born master of his sincere impressions, he was also a born horseman. He never appeared so happy or so much to advantage as on the back of a horse. He had formed the project of teaching my eldest boy to ride, and meantime, when the child was about two years old, presented him with his first dog.

I saw Stephen Crane a few days after his arrival in London. I saw him for the last time on his last day in England. It was in Dover, in a big hotel, in a bedroom with a large window looking on to the sea. He had been very ill and Mrs. Crane was taking him to some place in Germany, but one glance at that wasted face was enough to tell me that it was the most forlorn of all hopes. The last words he breathed out to me were: "I am tired. Give my love to your wife and child." When I stopped at the door for another look I saw that he had turned his head on the pillow and was staring wistfully out of the window at the sails of a cutter yacht that glided slowly across the frame, like a dim shadow against the grey sky.

Those who have read his little tale, "Horses," and the story, "The Open Boat," in the volume of that name, know with what fine understanding he loved horses and the sea. And his passage on this earth was like that of a horseman riding swiftly in the dawn of a day fated to be short and without sunshine.

TALES OF THE SEA—1898

It is by his irresistible power to reach the adventurous side in the character, not only of his own, but of all nations, that Marryat is largely human. He is the enslaver of youth, not by the literary artifices of presentation, but by the natural glamour of his own temperament. To his young heroes the beginning of life is a splendid and warlike lark, ending at last in inheritance and marriage. His novels are not the outcome of his art, but of his character, like the deeds that make up his record of naval service. To the artist his work is interesting as a completely successful expression of an unartistic nature. It is absolutely amazing to us, as the disclosure of the spirit animating the stirring time when the nineteenth century was young. There is an air of fable about it. Its loss would be irreparable, like the curtailment of national story or the loss of an historical document. It is the beginning and the embodiment of an inspiring tradition.

To this writer of the sea the sea was not an element. It was a stage, where was displayed an exhibition of valour, and of such achievement as the world had never seen before. The greatness of that achievement cannot be pronounced imaginary, since its reality has affected the destinies of nations; nevertheless, in its grandeur it has all the remoteness of an ideal. History preserves the skeleton of facts and, here and there, a figure or a name; but it is in Marryat's novels that we find the mass of the nameless, that we see them in the flesh, that we obtain a glimpse of the everyday life and an insight into the spirit animating the crowd of obscure men who knew how to build for their country such a shining monument of memories.

Marryat is really a writer of the Service. What sets him apart is his fidelity. His pen serves his country as well as did his professional skill and his renowned courage. His figures move about between water and sky, and the water and the sky are there only to frame the deeds of the Service. His novels, like amphibious creatures, live on the sea and frequent the shore, where they flounder deplorably. The loves and the hates of his boys are as primitive as their virtues and their vices. His women, from the beautiful Agnes to the witch-like mother of Lieutenant Vanslyperken, are, with the exception of the sailors' wives, like the shadows of what has never been. His Silvas, his Ribieras, his Shriftens, his Delmars remind us of people we have heard of somewhere, many times, without ever believing in their existence. His morality is honourable and conventional. There is cruelty in his fun and he can invent puns in the midst of carnage. His naiveties are perpetrated in a lurid light. There is an endless variety of types, all surface, with hard edges, with memorable eccentricities of outline, with a childish and heroic effect in the drawing. They do not belong to life; they belong exclusively to the Service. And yet they live; there is a truth in them, the truth of their time; a headlong, reckless audacity, an intimacy with violence, an unthinking fearlessness, and an exuberance of vitality which only years of war and victories can give. His adventures are enthralling; the rapidity of his action fascinates; his method is crude, his sentimentality, obviously incidental, is often factitious. His greatness is undeniable.

It is undeniable. To a multitude of readers the navy of to-day is Marryat's navy still. He has created a priceless legend. If he be not immortal, yet he will last long enough for the highest ambition, because he has dealt manfully with an inspiring phase in the history of that Service on which the life of his country depends. The tradition of the great past he has fixed in his pages will be cherished for ever as the guarantee of the future. He loved his country first, the Service next, the sea perhaps not at all. But the sea loved him without reserve. It gave him his professional distinction and his author's fame—a fame such as not often falls to the lot of a true artist.

At the same time, on the other side of the Atlantic, another man wrote of the sea with true artistic instinct. He is not invincibly young and heroic; he is mature and human, though for him also the stress of adventure and endeavour must end fatally in inheritance and marriage. For James Fenimore Cooper nature was not the frame-work, it was an essential part of existence. He could hear its voice, he could understand its silence, and he could interpret both for us in his prose with all that felicity and sureness of effect that belong to a poetical conception alone. His fame, as wide but less brilliant than that of his contemporary, rests mostly on a novel which is not of the sea. But he loved the sea and looked at it with consummate understanding. In his sea tales the sea inter-penetrates with life; it is in a subtle way a factor in the problem of existence, and, for all its greatness, it is always in touch with the men, who, bound on errands of war or gain, traverse its immense solitudes. His descriptions have the magistral ampleness of a gesture indicating the sweep of a vast horizon. They embrace the colours of sunset, the peace of starlight, the aspects of calm and storm, the great loneliness of the waters, the stillness of watchful coasts, and the alert readiness which marks men who live face to face with the promise and the menace of the sea.

He knows the men and he knows the sea. His method may be often faulty, but his art is genuine. The truth is within him. The road to legitimate realism is through poetical feeling, and he possesses that—only it is expressed in the leisurely manner of his time. He has the knowledge of simple hearts. Long Tom Coffin is a monumental seaman with the individuality of life and the significance of a type. It is hard to believe that Manual and Borroughcliffe, Mr. Marble of Marble-Head, Captain Tuck of the packet-ship *Montauk*, or Daggett, the tenacious commander of the *Sea Lion* of Martha's Vineyard, must pass away some day and be utterly forgotten. His sympathy is large, and his humour is as genuine—and as perfectly unaffected—as is his art. In certain passages he reaches, very simply, the heights of inspired vision.

He wrote before the great American language was born, and he wrote as well as any novelist of his time. If he pitches upon episodes redounding to the glory of the young republic, surely England has glory enough to forgive him, for the sake of his excellence, the patriotic bias at her expense. The interest of his tales is convincing and unflagging; and there runs through his work a steady vein of friendliness for the old country which the succeeding generations of his compatriots have replaced by a less definite sentiment.

Perhaps no two authors of fiction influenced so many lives and gave to so many the initial impulse towards a glorious or a useful career. Through the distances of space and time those two men of another race have shaped also the life of the writer of this appreciation. Life is life, and art is art—and truth is hard to find in either. Yet in testimony to the achievement of both these authors it may be said that, in the case of the writer at least, the youthful glamour, the headlong vitality of the one and the profound sympathy, the artistic insight of the other—to which he had surrendered—have withstood the brutal shock of facts and the wear of laborious years. He has never regretted his surrender.

AN OBSERVER IN MALAYA[3] —1898

In his new volume, Mr. Hugh Clifford, at the beginning of the sketch entitled "At the Heels of the White Man," expresses his anxiety as to the state of England's account in the Day-Book of the Recording Angel "for the good and the bad we have done—both with the most excellent intentions." The intentions will, no doubt, count for something, though, of course, every nation's conquests are paved with good intentions; or it may be that the Recording Angel, looking compassionately at the strife of hearts, may disdain to enter into the Eternal Book the facts of a struggle which has the reward of its righteousness even on this earth—in victory and lasting greatness, or in defeat and humiliation.

And, also, love will count for much. If the opinion of a looker-on from afar is worth anything, Mr. Hugh Clifford's anxiety about his country's record is needless. To the Malays whom he governs, instructs, and guides he is the embodiment of the intentions, of the conscience and might of his race. And of all the nations conquering distant territories in the name of the most excellent intentions, England alone sends out men who, with such a transparent sincerity of feeling, can speak, as Mr. Hugh Clifford does, of the place of toil and exile as "the land which is very dear to me, where the best years of my life have been spent"—and where (I would stake my right hand on it) his name is pronounced with respect and affection by those brown men about whom he writes.

All these studies are on a high level of interest, though not all on the same level. The descriptive chapters, results of personal observation, seem to me the most interesting. And, indeed, in a book of this kind it is the author's personality which awakens the greatest interest; it shapes itself before one in the ring of sentences, it is seen between the lines—like the progress of a traveller in the jungle that may be traced by the sound of the *parang* chopping the swaying creepers, while the man himself is glimpsed, now and then, indistinct and passing between the trees. Thus in his very vagueness of appearance, the writer seen through the leaves of his book becomes a fascinating companion in a land of fascination.

It is when dealing with the aspects of nature that Mr. Hugh Clifford is most convincing. He looks upon them lovingly, for the land is "very dear to him," and he records his cherished impressions so that the forest, the great flood, the jungle, the rapid river, and the menacing rock dwell in the memory of the reader long after the book is closed. He does not say anything, in so many words, of his affection for those who live amid the scenes he describes so well, but his humanity is large enough to pardon us if we suspect him of such a rare weakness. In his preface he expresses the regret at not having the gifts (whatever they may be) of the kailyard school, or—looking up to a very different plane— the genius of Mr. Barrie. He has, however, gifts of his own, and his genius has served his country and his fortunes in another direction. Yet it is when attempting what he professes himself unable to do, in telling us the simple story

---

[3] Studies in Brown Humanity. By Hugh Clifford.

of Umat, the punkah-puller, with unaffected simplicity and half-concealed tenderness, that he comes nearest to artistic achievement.

Each study in this volume presents some idea, illustrated by a fact told without artifice, but with an elective sureness of knowledge. The story of Tukang Burok's love, related in the old man's own words, conveys the very breath of Malay thought and speech. In "His Little Bill," the coolie, Lim Teng Wah, facing his debtor, stands very distinct before us, an insignificant and tragic victim of fate with whom he had quarrelled to the death over a matter of seven dollars and sixty-eight cents. The story of "The Schooner with a Past" may be heard, from the Straits eastward, with many variations. Out in the Pacific the schooner becomes a cutter, and the pearl-divers are replaced by the Black-birds of the Labour Trade. But Mr. Hugh Clifford's variation is very good. There is a passage in it—a trifle—just the diver as seen coming up from the depths, that in its dozen lines or so attains to distinct artistic value. And, scattered through the book, there are many other passages of almost equal descriptive excellence.

Nevertheless, to apply artistic standards to this book would be a fundamental error in appreciation. Like faith, enthusiasm, or heroism, art veils part of the truth of life to make the rest appear more splendid, inspiring, or sinister. And this book is only truth, interesting and futile, truth unadorned, simple and straightforward. The Resident of Pahang has the devoted friendship of Umat, the punkah-puller, he has an individual faculty of vision, a large sympathy, and the scrupulous consciousness of the good and evil in his hands. He may as well rest content with such gifts. One cannot expect to be, at the same time, a ruler of men and an irreproachable player on the flute.

A HAPPY WANDERER—1910

Converts are interesting people. Most of us, if you will pardon me for betraying the universal secret, have, at some time or other, discovered in ourselves a readiness to stray far, ever so far, on the wrong road. And what did we do in our pride and our cowardice? Casting fearful glances and waiting for a dark moment, we buried our discovery discreetly, and kept on in the old direction, on that old, beaten track we have not had courage enough to leave, and which we perceive now more clearly than before to be but the arid way of the grave.

The convert, the man capable of grace (I am speaking here in a secular sense), is not discreet. His pride is of another kind; he jumps gladly off the track—the touch of grace is mostly sudden—and facing about in a new direction may even attain the illusion of having turned his back on Death itself.

Some converts have, indeed, earned immortality by their exquisite indiscretion. The most illustrious example of a convert, that Flower of chivalry, Don Quixote de la Mancha, remains for all the world the only genuine immortal hidalgo. The delectable Knight of Spain became converted, as you know, from the ways of a small country squire to an imperative faith in a tender and sublime mission. Forthwith he was beaten with sticks and in due course shut up in a wooden cage by the Barber and the Priest, the fit ministers of a justly shocked social order. I do not know if it has occurred to anybody yet to shut up Mr. Luffmann in a wooden cage.[4] I do not raise the point because I wish him any harm. Quite the contrary. I am a humane person. Let him take it as the highest praise—but I must say that he richly deserves that sort of attention.

On the other hand I would not have him unduly puffed up with the pride of the exalted association. The grave wisdom, the admirable amenity, the serene grace of the secular patron-saint of all mortals converted to noble visions are not his. Mr. Luffmann has no mission. He is no Knight sublimely Errant. But he is an excellent Vagabond. He is full of merit. That peripatetic guide, philosopher and friend of all nations, Mr. Roosevelt, would promptly excommunicate him with a big stick. The truth is that the ex-autocrat of all the States does not like rebels against the sullen order of our universe. Make the best of it or perish—he cries. A sane lineal successor of the Barber and the Priest, and a sagacious political heir of the incomparable Sancho Panza (another great Governor), that distinguished litterateur has no mercy for dreamers. And our author happens to be a man of (you may trace them in his books) some rather fine reveries.

Every convert begins by being a rebel, and I do not see myself how any mercy can possibly be extended to Mr. Luffmann. He is a convert from the creed of strenuous life. For this renegade the body is of little account; to him work appears criminal when it suppresses the demands of the inner life; while he was young he did grind virtuously at the sacred handle, and now, he says, he has fallen into disgrace with some people because he believes no longer in toil

---

[4] *Quiet Days in Spain.* By C. Bogue Luffmann.

without end. Certain respectable folk hate him—so he says—because he dares to think that "poetry, beauty, and the broad face of the world are the best things to be in love with." He confesses to loving Spain on the ground that she is "the land of to-morrow, and holds the gospel of never-mind." The universal striving to push ahead he considers mere vulgar folly. Didn't I tell you he was a fit subject for the cage?

It is a relief (we are all humane, are we not?) to discover that this desperate character is not altogether an outcast. Little girls seem to like him. One of them, after listening to some of his tales, remarked to her mother, "Wouldn't it be lovely if what he says were true!" Here you have Woman! The charming creatures will neither strain at a camel nor swallow a gnat. Not publicly. These operations, without which the world they have such a large share in could not go on for ten minutes, are left to us—men. And then we are chided for being coarse. This is a refined objection but does not seem fair. Another little girl—or perhaps the same little girl—wrote to him in Cordova, "I hope Poste-Restante is a nice place, and that you are very comfortable." Woman again! I have in my time told some stories which are (I hate false modesty) both true and lovely. Yet no little girl ever wrote to me in kindly terms. And why? Simply because I am not enough of a Vagabond. The dear despots of the fireside have a weakness for lawless characters. This is amiable, but does not seem rational.

Being Quixotic, Mr. Luffmann is no Impressionist. He is far too earnest in his heart, and not half sufficiently precise in his style to be that. But he is an excellent narrator. More than any Vagabond I have ever met, he knows what he is about. There is not one of his quiet days which is dull. You will find in them a love-story not made up, the *coup-de-foudre*, the lightning-stroke of Spanish love; and you will marvel how a spell so sudden and vehement can be at the same time so tragically delicate. You will find there landladies devoured with jealousy, astute housekeepers, delightful boys, wise peasants, touchy shopkeepers, all the *cosas de Espana*—and, in addition, the pale girl Rosario. I recommend that pathetic and silent victim of fate to your benevolent compassion. You will find in his pages the humours of starving workers of the soil, the vision among the mountains of an exulting mad spirit in a mighty body, and many other visions worthy of attention. And they are exact visions, for this idealist is no visionary. He is in sympathy with suffering mankind, and has a grasp on real human affairs. I mean the great and pitiful affairs concerned with bread, love, and the obscure, unexpressed needs which drive great crowds to prayer in the holy places of the earth.

But I like his conception of what a "quiet" life is like! His quiet days require no fewer than forty-two of the forty-nine provinces of Spain to take their ease in. For his unquiet days, I presume, the seven—or is it nine?—crystal spheres of Alexandrian cosmogony would afford, but a wretchedly straitened space. A most unconventional thing is his notion of quietness. One would take it as a joke; only that, perchance, to the author of *Quiet Days in Spain* all days may seem quiet, because, a courageous convert, he is now at peace with himself.

How better can we take leave of this interesting Vagabond than with the road salutation of passing wayfarers: "And on you be peace! . . . You have chosen your ideal, and it is a good choice. There's nothing like giving up one's life to an unselfish passion. Let the rich and the powerful of this globe preach their sound gospel of palpable progress. The part of the ideal you embrace is the better one, if only in its illusions. No great passion can be barren. May a world of gracious and poignant images attend the lofty solitude of your renunciation!"

THE LIFE BEYOND—1910

You have no doubt noticed that certain books produce a sort of physical effect on one—mostly an audible effect. I am not alluding here to Blue books or to books of statistics. The effect of these is simply exasperating and no more. No! the books I have in mind are just the common books of commerce you and I read when we have five minutes to spare, the usual hired books published by ordinary publishers, printed by ordinary printers, and censored (when they happen to be novels) by the usual circulating libraries, the guardians of our firesides, whose names are household words within the four seas.

To see the fair and the brave of this free country surrendering themselves with unbounded trust to the direction of the circulating libraries is very touching. It is even, in a sense, a beautiful spectacle, because, as you know, humility is a rare and fragrant virtue; and what can be more humble than to surrender your morals and your intellect to the judgment of one of your tradesmen? I suppose that there are some very perfect people who allow the Army and Navy Stores to censor their diet. So much merit, however, I imagine, is not frequently met with here below. The flesh, alas! is weak, and—from a certain point of view—so important!

A superficial person might be rendered miserable by the simple question: What would become of us if the circulating libraries ceased to exist? It is a horrid and almost indelicate supposition, but let us be brave and face the truth. On this earth of ours nothing lasts. *Tout passe, tout casse, tout lasse.* Imagine the utter wreck overtaking the morals of our beautiful country-houses should the circulating libraries suddenly die! But pray do not shudder. There is no occasion.

Their spirit shall survive. I declare this from inward conviction, and also from scientific information received lately. For observe: the circulating libraries are human institutions. I beg you to follow me closely. They are human institutions, and being human, they are not animal, and, therefore, they are spiritual. Thus, any man with enough money to take a shop, stock his shelves, and pay for advertisements shall be able to evoke the pure and censorious spectre of the circulating libraries whenever his own commercial spirit moves him.

For, and this is the information alluded to above, Science, having in its infinite wanderings run up against various wonders and mysteries, is apparently willing now to allow a spiritual quality to man and, I conclude, to all his works as well.

I do not know exactly what this "Science" may be; and I do not think that anybody else knows; but that is the information stated shortly. It is contained in a book reposing under my thoughtful eyes.[5] I know it is not a censored book, because I can see for myself that it is not a novel. The author, on his side, warns me that it is not philosophy, that it is not metaphysics, that it is not natural

---

[5] Existence after Death Implied by Science. By Jasper B. Hunt, M.A.

science. After this comprehensive warning, the definition of the book becomes, you will admit, a pretty hard nut to crack.

But meantime let us return for a moment to my opening remark about the physical effect of some common, hired books. A few of them (not necessarily books of verse) are melodious; the music some others make for you as you read has the disagreeable emphasis of a barrel-organ; the tinkling-cymbals book (it was not written by a humorist) I only met once. But there is infinite variety in the noises books do make. I have now on my shelves a book apparently of the most valuable kind which, before I have read half-a-dozen lines, begins to make a noise like a buzz-saw. I am inconsolable; I shall never, I fear, discover what it is all about, for the buzzing covers the words, and at every try I am absolutely forced to give it up ere the end of the page is reached.

The book, however, which I have found so difficult to define, is by no means noisy. As a mere piece of writing it may be described as being breathless itself and taking the reader's breath away, not by the magnitude of its message but by a sort of anxious volubility in the delivery. The constantly elusive argument and the illustrative quotations go on without a single reflective pause. For this reason alone the reading of that work is a fatiguing process.

The author himself (I use his own words) "suspects" that what he has written "may be theology after all." It may be. It is not my place either to allay or to confirm the author's suspicion of his own work. But I will state its main thesis: "That science regarded in the gross dictates the spirituality of man and strongly implies a spiritual destiny for individual human beings." This means: Existence after Death—that is, Immortality.

To find out its value you must go to the book. But I will observe here that an Immortality liable at any moment to betray itself fatuously by the forcible incantations of Mr. Stead or Professor Crookes is scarcely worth having. Can you imagine anything more squalid than an Immortality at the beck and call of Eusapia Palladino? That woman lives on the top floor of a Neapolitan house, and gets our poor, pitiful, august dead, flesh of our flesh, bone of our bone, spirit of our spirit, who have loved, suffered and died, as we must love, suffer, and die—she gets them to beat tambourines in a corner and protrude shadowy limbs through a curtain. This is particularly horrible, because, if one had to put one's faith in these things one could not even die safely from disgust, as one would long to do.

And to believe that these manifestations, which the author evidently takes for modern miracles, will stay our tottering faith; to believe that the new psychology has, only the other day, discovered man to be a "spiritual mystery," is really carrying humility towards that universal provider, Science, too far.

We moderns have complicated our old perplexities to the point of absurdity; our perplexities older than religion itself. It is not for nothing that for so many centuries the priest, mounting the steps of the altar, murmurs, "Why art thou sad, my soul, and why dost thou trouble me?" Since the day of Creation two veiled figures, Doubt and Melancholy, are pacing endlessly in the sunshine of the world. What humanity needs is not the promise of scientific immortality, but compassionate pity in this life and infinite mercy on the Day of Judgment.

And, for the rest, during this transient hour of our pilgrimage, we may well be content to repeat the Invocation of Sar Peladan. Sar Peladan was an occultist, a seer, a modern magician. He believed in astrology, in the spirits of the air, in elves; he was marvellously and deliciously absurd. Incidentally he wrote some incomprehensible poems and a few pages of harmonious prose, for, you must know, "a magician is nothing else but a great harmonist." Here are some eight lines of the magnificent Invocation. Let me, however, warn you, strictly between ourselves, that my translation is execrable. I am sorry to say I am no magician.

"O Nature, indulgent Mother, forgive! Open your arms to the son, prodigal and weary.

"I have attempted to tear asunder the veil you have hung to conceal from us the pain of life, and I have been wounded by the mystery. . . . OEdipus, half way to finding the word of the enigma, young Faust, regretting already the simple life, the life of the heart, I come back to you repentant, reconciled, O gentle deceiver!"

THE ASCENDING EFFORT—1910

Much good paper has been lamentably wasted to prove that science has destroyed, that it is destroying, or, some day, may destroy poetry. Meantime, unblushing, unseen, and often unheard, the guileless poets have gone on singing in a sweet strain. How they dare do the impossible and virtually forbidden thing is a cause for wonder but not for legislation. Not yet. We are at present too busy reforming the silent burglar and planning concerts to soothe the savage breast of the yelling hooligan. As somebody—perhaps a publisher—said lately: "Poetry is of no account now- a-days."

But it is not totally neglected. Those persons with gold-rimmed spectacles whose usual occupation is to spy upon the obvious have remarked audibly (on several occasions) that poetry has so far not given to science any acknowledgment worthy of its distinguished position in the popular mind. Except that Tennyson looked down the throat of a foxglove, that Erasmus Darwin wrote *The Loves of the Plants* and a scoffer *The Loves of the Triangles*, poets have been supposed to be indecorously blind to the progress of science. What tribute, for instance, has poetry paid to electricity? All I can remember on the spur of the moment is Mr. Arthur Symons' line about arc lamps: "Hung with the globes of some unnatural fruit."

Commerce and Manufacture praise on every hand in their not mute but inarticulate way the glories of science. Poetry does not play its part. Behold John Keats, skilful with the surgeon's knife; but when he writes poetry his inspiration is not from the operating table. Here I am reminded, though, of a modern instance to the contrary in prose. Mr. H. G. Wells, who, as far as I know, has never written a line of verse, was inspired a few years ago to write a short story, *Under the Knife*. Out of a clock-dial, a brass rod, and a whiff of chloroform, he has conjured for us a sensation of space and eternity, evoked the face of the Unknowable, and an awesome, august voice, like the voice of the Judgment Day; a great voice, perhaps the voice of science itself, uttering the words: "There shall be no more pain!" I advise you to look up that story, so human and so intimate, because Mr. Wells, the writer of prose whose amazing inventiveness we all know, remains a poet even in his most perverse moments of scorn for things as they are. His poetic imagination is sometimes even greater than his inventiveness, I am not afraid to say. But, indeed, imaginative faculty would make any man a poet—were he born without tongue for speech and without hands to seize his fancy and fasten her down to a wretched piece of paper.

The book[6] which in the course of the last few days I have opened and shut several times is not imaginative. But, on the other hand, it is not a dumb book, as some are. It has even a sort of sober and serious eloquence, reminding us that not poetry alone is at fault in this matter. Mr. Bourne begins his *Ascending Effort*

---

[6] *The Ascending Effort*. By George Bourne.

with a remark by Sir Francis Galton upon Eugenics that "if the principles he was advocating were to become effective they must be introduced into the national conscience, like a new religion." "Introduced" suggests compulsory vaccination. Mr. Bourne, who is not a theologian, wishes to league together not science and religion, but science and the arts. "The intoxicating power of art," he thinks, is the very thing needed to give the desired effect to the doctrines of science. In uninspired phrase he points to the arts playing once upon a time a part in "popularising the Christian tenets." With painstaking fervour as great as the fervour of prophets, but not so persuasive, he foresees the arts some day popularising science. Until that day dawns, science will continue to be lame and poetry blind. He himself cannot smooth or even point out the way, though he thinks that "a really prudent people would be greedy of beauty," and their public authorities "as careful of the sense of comfort as of sanitation."

As the writer of those remarkable rustic note-books, *The Bettesworth Book* and *Memoirs of a Surrey Labourer*, the author has a claim upon our attention. But his seriousness, his patience, his almost touching sincerity, can only command the respect of his readers and nothing more. He is obsessed by science, haunted and shadowed by it, until he has been bewildered into awe. He knows, indeed, that art owes its triumphs and its subtle influence to the fact that it issues straight from our organic vitality, and is a movement of life-cells with their matchless unintellectual knowledge. But the fact that poetry does not seem obviously in love with science has never made him doubt whether it may not be an argument against his haste to see the marriage ceremony performed amid public rejoicings.

Many a man has heard or read and believes that the earth goes round the sun; one small blob of mud among several others, spinning ridiculously with a waggling motion like a top about to fall. This is the Copernican system, and the man believes in the system without often knowing as much about it as its name. But while watching a sunset he sheds his belief; he sees the sun as a small and useful object, the servant of his needs and the witness of his ascending effort, sinking slowly behind a range of mountains, and then he holds the system of Ptolemy. He holds it without knowing it. In the same way a poet hears, reads, and believes a thousand undeniable truths which have not yet got into his blood, nor will do after reading Mr. Bourne's book; he writes, therefore, as if neither truths nor book existed. Life and the arts follow dark courses, and will not turn aside to the brilliant arc-lights of science. Some day, without a doubt,—and it may be a consolation to Mr. Bourne to know it—fully informed critics will point out that Mr. Davies's poem on a dark woman combing her hair must have been written after the invasion of appendicitis, and that Mr. Yeats's "Had I the heaven's embroidered cloths" came before radium was quite unnecessarily dragged out of its respectable obscurity in pitchblende to upset the venerable (and comparatively naive) chemistry of our young days.

There are times when the tyranny of science and the cant of science are alarming, but there are other times when they are entertaining—and this is one of them. "Many a man prides himself" says Mr. Bourne, "on his piety or his views of art, whose whole range of ideas, could they be investigated, would be found ordinary, if not base, because they have been adopted in compliance with some external persuasion or to serve some timid purpose instead of proceeding authoritatively from the living selection of his hereditary taste." This extract is a fair sample of the book's thought and of its style. But Mr. Bourne seems to forget that "persuasion" is a vain thing. The appreciation of great art comes from within.

It is but the merest justice to say that the transparent honesty of Mr. Bourne's purpose is undeniable. But the whole book is simply an earnest expression of a pious wish; and, like the generality of pious wishes, this one seems of little dynamic value—besides being impracticable.

Yes, indeed. Art has served Religion; artists have found the most exalted inspiration in Christianity; but the light of Transfiguration which has illuminated the profoundest mysteries of our sinful souls is not the light of the generating stations, which exposes the depths of our infatuation where our mere cleverness is permitted for a while to grope for the unessential among invincible shadows.

THE CENSOR OF PLAYS—AN APPRECIATION—1907

A couple of years ago I was moved to write a one-act play—and I lived long enough to accomplish the task. We live and learn. When the play was finished I was informed that it had to be licensed for performance. Thus I learned of the existence of the Censor of Plays. I may say without vanity that I am intelligent enough to have been astonished by that piece of information: for facts must stand in some relation to time and space, and I was aware of being in England— in the twentieth-century England. The fact did not fit the date and the place. That was my first thought. It was, in short, an improper fact. I beg you to believe that I am writing in all seriousness and am weighing my words scrupulously.

Therefore I don't say inappropriate. I say improper—that is: something to be ashamed of. And at first this impression was confirmed by the obscurity in which the figure embodying this after all considerable fact had its being. The Censor of Plays! His name was not in the mouths of all men. Far from it. He seemed stealthy and remote. There was about that figure the scent of the far East, like the peculiar atmosphere of a Mandarin's back yard, and the mustiness of the Middle Ages, that epoch when mankind tried to stand still in a monstrous illusion of final certitude attained in morals, intellect and conscience.

It was a disagreeable impression. But I reflected that probably the censorship of plays was an inactive monstrosity; not exactly a survival, since it seemed obviously at variance with the genius of the people, but an heirloom of past ages, a bizarre and imported curiosity preserved because of that weakness one has for one's old possessions apart from any intrinsic value; one more object of exotic *virtu*, an Oriental *potiche*, a *magot chinois* conceived by a childish and extravagant imagination, but allowed to stand in stolid impotence in the twilight of the upper shelf.

Thus I quieted my uneasy mind. Its uneasiness had nothing to do with the fate of my one-act play. The play was duly produced, and an exceptionally intelligent audience stared it coldly off the boards. It ceased to exist. It was a fair and open execution. But having survived the freezing atmosphere of that auditorium I continued to exist, labouring under no sense of wrong. I was not pleased, but I was content. I was content to accept the verdict of a free and independent public, judging after its conscience the work of its free, independent and conscientious servant—the artist.

Only thus can the dignity of artistic servitude be preserved—not to speak of the bare existence of the artist and the self-respect of the man. I shall say nothing of the self-respect of the public. To the self- respect of the public the present appeal against the censorship is being made and I join in it with all my heart.

For I have lived long enough to learn that the monstrous and outlandish figure, the *magot chinois* whom I believed to be but a memorial of our forefathers' mental aberration, that grotesque *potiche*, works! The absurd and hollow creature of clay seems to be alive with a sort of (surely) unconscious life worthy of its traditions. It heaves its stomach, it rolls its eyes, it brandishes a monstrous arm: and with the censorship, like a Bravo of old Venice with a more carnal weapon, stabs its victim from behind in the twilight of its upper shelf. Less picturesque than the Venetian in cloak and mask, less estimable, too, in this, that the assassin plied his moral trade at his own risk deriving no countenance from the powers of the Republic, it stands more malevolent, inasmuch that the Bravo striking in the dusk killed but the body, whereas the grotesque thing nodding its mandarin head may in its absurd unconsciousness strike down at any time the spirit of an honest, of an artistic, perhaps of a sublime creation.

This Chinese monstrosity, disguised in the trousers of the Western Barbarian and provided by the State with the immortal Mr. Stiggins's plug hat and umbrella, is with us. It is an office. An office of trust. And from time to time there is found an official to fill it. He is a public man. The least prominent of public men, the most unobtrusive, the most obscure if not the most modest.

But however obscure, a public man may be told the truth if only once in his life. His office flourishes in the shade; not in the rustic shade beloved of the violet but in the muddled twilight of mind, where tyranny of every sort flourishes. Its holder need not have either brain or heart, no sight, no taste, no imagination, not even bowels of compassion. He needs not these things. He has power. He can kill thought, and incidentally truth, and incidentally beauty, providing they seek to live in a dramatic form. He can do it, without seeing, without understanding, without feeling anything; out of mere stupid suspicion, as an irresponsible Roman Caesar could kill a senator. He can do that and there is no one to say him nay. He may call his cook (Moliere used to do that) from below and give her five acts to judge every morning as a matter of constant practice and still remain the unquestioned destroyer of men's honest work. He may have a glass too much. This accident has happened to persons of unimpeachable morality—to gentlemen. He may suffer from spells of imbecility like Clodius. He may . . . what might he not do! I tell you he is the Caesar of the dramatic world. There has been since the Roman Principate nothing in the way of irresponsible power to compare with the office of the Censor of Plays.

Looked at in this way it has some grandeur, something colossal in the odious and the absurd. This figure in whose power it is to suppress an intellectual conception—to kill thought (a dream for a mad brain, my masters!)—seems designed in a spirit of bitter comedy to bring out the greatness of a Philistine's conceit and his moral cowardice.

But this is England in the twentieth century, and one wonders that there can be found a man courageous enough to occupy the post. It is a matter for meditation. Having given it a few minutes I come to the conclusion in the serenity of my heart and the peace of my conscience that he must be either an extreme megalomaniac or an utterly unconscious being.

He must be unconscious. It is one of the qualifications for his magistracy. Other qualifications are equally easy. He must have done nothing, expressed nothing, imagined nothing. He must be obscure, insignificant and mediocre—in thought, act, speech and sympathy. He must know nothing of art, of life—and of himself. For if he did he would not dare to be what he is. Like that much questioned and mysterious bird, the phoenix, he sits amongst the cold ashes of his predecessor upon the altar of morality, alone of his kind in the sight of wondering generations.

And I will end with a quotation reproducing not perhaps the exact words but the true spirit of a lofty conscience.

"Often when sitting down to write the notice of a play, especially when I felt it antagonistic to my canons of art, to my tastes or my convictions, I hesitated in the fear lest my conscientious blame might check the development of a great talent, my sincere judgment condemn a worthy mind. With the pen poised in my hand I hesitated, whispering to myself 'What if I were perchance doing my part in killing a masterpiece.'"

Such were the lofty scruples of M. Jules Lemaitre—dramatist and dramatic critic, a great citizen and a high magistrate in the Republic of Letters; a Censor of Plays exercising his august office openly in the light of day, with the authority of a European reputation. But then M. Jules Lemaitre is a man possessed of wisdom, of great fame, of a fine conscience—not an obscure hollow Chinese monstrosity ornamented with Mr. Stiggins's plug hat and cotton umbrella by its anxious grandmother—the State.

Frankly, is it not time to knock the improper object off its shelf? It has stood too long there. Hatched in Pekin (I should say) by some Board of Respectable Rites, the little caravan monster has come to us by way of Moscow—I suppose. It is outlandish. It is not venerable. It does not belong here. Is it not time to knock it off its dark shelf with some implement appropriate to its worth and status? With an old broom handle for instance.

PART II—LIFE

AUTOCRACY AND WAR—1905

From the firing of the first shot on the banks of the Sha-ho, the fate of the great battle of the Russo-Japanese war hung in the balance for more than a fortnight. The famous three-day battles, for which history has reserved the recognition of special pages, sink into insignificance before the struggles in Manchuria engaging half a million men on fronts of sixty miles, struggles lasting for weeks, flaming up fiercely and dying away from sheer exhaustion, to flame up again in desperate persistence, and end—as we have seen them end more than once—not from the victor obtaining a crushing advantage, but through the mortal weariness of the combatants.

We have seen these things, though we have seen them only in the cold, silent, colourless print of books and newspapers. In stigmatising the printed word as cold, silent and colourless, I have no intention of putting a slight upon the fidelity and the talents of men who have provided us with words to read about the battles in Manchuria. I only wished to suggest that in the nature of things, the war in the Far East has been made known to us, so far, in a grey reflection of its terrible and monotonous phases of pain, death, sickness; a reflection seen in the perspective of thousands of miles, in the dim atmosphere of official reticence, through the veil of inadequate words. Inadequate, I say, because what had to be reproduced is beyond the common experience of war, and our imagination, luckily for our peace of mind, has remained a slumbering faculty, notwithstanding the din of humanitarian talk and the real progress of humanitarian ideas. Direct vision of the fact, or the stimulus of a great art, can alone make it turn and open its eyes heavy with blessed sleep; and even there, as against the testimony of the senses and the stirring up of emotion, that saving callousness which reconciles us to the conditions of our existence, will assert itself under the guise of assent to fatal necessity, or in the enthusiasm of a purely aesthetic admiration of the rendering. In this age of knowledge our sympathetic imagination, to which alone we can look for the ultimate triumph of concord and justice, remains strangely impervious to information, however correctly and even picturesquely conveyed. As to the vaunted eloquence of a serried array of figures, it has all the futility of precision without force. It is the exploded superstition of enthusiastic statisticians. An over-worked horse falling in front of our windows, a man writhing under a cart-wheel in the streets awaken more genuine emotion, more horror, pity, and indignation than the stream of reports, appalling in their monotony, of tens of thousands of decaying bodies tainting the air of the Manchurian plains, of other tens of thousands of maimed bodies groaning in ditches, crawling on the frozen ground, filling the field hospitals; of the hundreds of thousands of survivors no less pathetic and even more tragic in being left alive by fate to the wretched exhaustion of their pitiful toil.

An early Victorian, or perhaps a pre-Victorian, sentimentalist, looking out of an upstairs window, I believe, at a street—perhaps Fleet Street itself—full of people, is reported, by an admiring friend, to have wept for joy at seeing so much life. These arcadian tears, this facile emotion worthy of the golden age, comes to us from the past, with solemn approval, after the close of the Napoleonic wars and before the series of sanguinary surprises held in reserve by the nineteenth century for our hopeful grandfathers. We may well envy them their optimism of which this anecdote of an amiable wit and sentimentalist presents an extreme instance, but still, a true instance, and worthy of regard in the spontaneous testimony to that trust in the life of the earth, triumphant at last in the felicity of her children. Moreover, the psychology of individuals, even in the most extreme instances, reflects the general effect of the fears and hopes of its time. Wept for joy! I should think that now, after eighty years, the emotion would be of a sterner sort. One could not imagine anybody shedding tears of joy at the sight of much life in a street, unless, perhaps, he were an enthusiastic officer of a general staff or a popular politician, with a career yet to make. And hardly even that. In the case of the first tears would be unprofessional, and a stern repression of all signs of joy at the provision of so much food for powder more in accord with the rules of prudence; the joy of the second would be checked before it found issue in weeping by anxious doubts as to the soundness of these electors' views upon the question of the hour, and the fear of missing the consensus of their votes.

No! It seems that such a tender joy would be misplaced now as much as ever during the last hundred years, to go no further back. The end of the eighteenth century was, too, a time of optimism and of dismal mediocrity in which the French Revolution exploded like a bombshell. In its lurid blaze the insufficiency of Europe, the inferiority of minds, of military and administrative systems, stood exposed with pitiless vividness. And there is but little courage in saying at this time of the day that the glorified French Revolution itself, except for its destructive force, was in essentials a mediocre phenomenon. The parentage of that great social and political upheaval was intellectual, the idea was elevated; but it is the bitter fate of any idea to lose its royal form and power, to lose its "virtue" the moment it descends from its solitary throne to work its will among the people. It is a king whose destiny is never to know the obedience of his subjects except at the cost of degradation. The degradation of the ideas of freedom and justice at the root of the French Revolution is made manifest in the person of its heir; a personality without law or faith, whom it has been the fashion to represent as an eagle, but who was, in truth, more like a sort of vulture preying upon the body of a Europe which did, indeed, for some dozen of years, very much resemble a corpse. The subtle and manifold influence for evil of the Napoleonic episode as a school of violence, as a sower of national hatreds, as the direct provocator of obscurantism and reaction, of political tyranny and injustice, cannot well be exaggerated.

The nineteenth century began with wars which were the issue of a corrupted revolution. It may be said that the twentieth begins with a war which is like the explosive ferment of a moral grave, whence may yet emerge a new political organism to take the place of a gigantic and dreaded phantom. For a hundred years the ghost of Russian might, overshadowing with its fantastic bulk the councils of Central and Western Europe, sat upon the gravestone of autocracy, cutting off from air, from light, from all knowledge of themselves and of the world, the buried millions of Russian people. Not the most determined cockney sentimentalist could have had the heart to weep for joy at the thought of its teeming numbers! And yet they were living, they are alive yet, since, through the mist of print, we have seen their blood freezing crimson upon the snow of the squares and streets of St. Petersburg; since their generations born in the grave are yet alive enough to fill the ditches and cover the fields of Manchuria with their torn limbs; to send up from the frozen ground of battlefields a chorus of groans calling for vengeance from Heaven; to kill and retreat, or kill and advance, without intermission or rest for twenty hours, for fifty hours, for whole weeks of fatigue, hunger, cold, and murder—till their ghastly labour, worthy of a place amongst the punishments of Dante's Inferno, passing through the stages of courage, of fury, of hopelessness, sinks into the night of crazy despair.

It seems that in both armies many men are driven beyond the bounds of sanity by the stress of moral and physical misery. Great numbers of soldiers and regimental officers go mad as if by way of protest against the peculiar sanity of a state of war: mostly among the Russians, of course. The Japanese have in their favour the tonic effect of success; and the innate gentleness of their character stands them in good stead. But the Japanese grand army has yet another advantage in this nerve-destroying contest, which for endless, arduous toil of killing surpasses all the wars of history. It has a base for its operations; a base of a nature beyond the concern of the many books written upon the so- called art of war, which, considered by itself, purely as an exercise of human ingenuity, is at best only a thing of well-worn, simple artifices. The Japanese army has for its base a reasoned conviction; it has behind it the profound belief in the right of a logical necessity to be appeased at the cost of so much blood and treasure. And in that belief, whether well or ill founded, that army stands on the high ground of conscious assent, shouldering deliberately the burden of a long-tried faithfulness. The other people (since each people is an army nowadays), torn out from a miserable quietude resembling death itself, hurled across space, amazed, without starting-point of its own or knowledge of the aim, can feel nothing but a horror-stricken consciousness of having mysteriously become the plaything of a black and merciless fate.

The profound, the instructive nature of this war is resumed by the memorable difference in the spiritual state of the two armies; the one forlorn and dazed on being driven out from an abyss of mental darkness into the red light of a conflagration, the other with a full knowledge of its past and its future, "finding itself" as it were at every step of the trying war before the eyes of an astonished world. The greatness of the lesson has been dwarfed for most of us by an often half-conscious prejudice of race-difference. The West having managed to lodge its hasty foot on the neck of the East, is prone to forget that it is from the East that the wonders of patience and wisdom have come to a world of men who set the value of life in the power to act rather than in the faculty of meditation. It has been dwarfed by this, and it has been obscured by a cloud of considerations with whose shaping wisdom and meditation had little or nothing to do; by the weary platitudes on the military situation which (apart from geographical conditions) is the same everlasting situation that has prevailed since the times of Hannibal and Scipio, and further back yet, since the beginning of historical record—since prehistoric times, for that matter; by the conventional expressions of horror at the tale of maiming and killing; by the rumours of peace with guesses more or less plausible as to its conditions. All this is made legitimate by the consecrated custom of writers in such time as this—the time of a great war. More legitimate in view of the situation created in Europe are the speculations as to the course of events after the war. More legitimate, but hardly more wise than the irresponsible talk of strategy that never changes, and of terms of peace that do not matter.

And above it all—unaccountably persistent—the decrepit, old, hundred years old, spectre of Russia's might still faces Europe from across the teeming graves of Russian people. This dreaded and strange apparition, bristling with bayonets, armed with chains, hung over with holy images; that something not of this world, partaking of a ravenous ghoul, of a blind Djinn grown up from a cloud, and of the Old Man of the Sea, still faces us with its old stupidity, with its strange mystical arrogance, stamping its shadowy feet upon the gravestone of autocracy already cracked beyond repair by the torpedoes of Togo and the guns of Oyama, already heaving in the blood-soaked ground with the first stirrings of a resurrection.

Never before had the Western world the opportunity to look so deep into the black abyss which separates a soulless autocracy posing as, and even believing itself to be, the arbiter of Europe, from the benighted, starved souls of its people. This is the real object-lesson of this war, its unforgettable information. And this war's true mission, disengaged from the economic origins of that contest, from doors open or shut, from the fields of Korea for Russian wheat or Japanese rice, from the ownership of ice-free ports and the command of the waters of the East—its true mission was to lay a ghost. It has accomplished it. Whether Kuropatkin was incapable or unlucky, whether or not Russia issuing next year, or the year after next, from behind a rampart of piled-up corpses will win or lose a fresh campaign, are minor considerations. The task of Japan is done, the mission accomplished; the ghost of Russia's might is laid. Only Europe, accustomed so long to the presence of that portent, seems unable to comprehend that, as in the fables of our childhood, the twelve strokes of the hour have rung, the cock has crowed, the apparition has vanished—never to haunt again this world which has been used to gaze at it with vague dread and many misgivings.

It was a fascination. And the hallucination still lasts as inexplicable in its persistence as in its duration. It seems so unaccountable, that the doubt arises as to the sincerity of all that talk as to what Russia will or will not do, whether it will raise or not another army, whether it will bury the Japanese in Manchuria under seventy millions of sacrificed peasants' caps (as her Press boasted a little more than a year ago) or give up to Japan that jewel of her crown, Saghalien, together with some other things; whether, perchance, as an interesting alternative, it will make peace on the Amur in order to make war beyond the Oxus.

All these speculations (with many others) have appeared gravely in print; and if they have been gravely considered by only one reader out of each hundred, there must be something subtly noxious to the human brain in the composition of newspaper ink; or else it is that the large page, the columns of words, the leaded headings, exalt the mind into a state of feverish credulity. The printed page of the Press makes a sort of still uproar, taking from men both the power to reflect and the faculty of genuine feeling; leaving them only the artificially created need of having something exciting to talk about.

The truth is that the Russia of our fathers, of our childhood, of our middle-age; the testamentary Russia of Peter the Great—who imagined that all the nations were delivered into the hand of Tsardom—can do nothing. It can do nothing because it does not exist. It has vanished for ever at last, and as yet there is no new Russia to take the place of that ill- omened creation, which, being a fantasy of a madman's brain, could in reality be nothing else than a figure out of a nightmare seated upon a monument of fear and oppression.

The true greatness of a State does not spring from such a contemptible source. It is a matter of logical growth, of faith and courage. Its inspiration springs from the constructive instinct of the people, governed by the strong hand of a collective conscience and voiced in the wisdom and counsel of men who seldom reap the reward of gratitude. Many States have been powerful, but, perhaps, none have been truly great—as yet. That the position of a State in reference to the moral methods of its development can be seen only historically, is true. Perhaps mankind has not lived long enough for a comprehensive view of any particular case. Perhaps no one will ever live long enough; and perhaps this earth shared out amongst our clashing ambitions by the anxious arrangements of statesmen will come to an end before we attain the felicity of greeting with unanimous applause the perfect fruition of a great State. It is even possible that we are destined for another sort of bliss altogether: that sort which consists in being perpetually duped by false appearances. But whatever political illusion the future may hold out to our fear or our admiration, there will be none, it is safe to say, which in the magnitude of anti-humanitarian effect will equal that phantom now driven out of the world by the thunder of thousands of guns; none that in its retreat will cling with an equally shameless sincerity to more unworthy supports: to the moral corruption and mental darkness of slavery, to the mere brute force of numbers.

This very ignominy of infatuation should make clear to men's feelings and reason that the downfall of Russia's might is unavoidable. Spectral it lived and spectral it disappears without leaving a memory of a single generous deed, of a single service rendered—even involuntarily—to the polity of nations. Other despotisms there have been, but none whose origin was so grimly fantastic in its baseness, and the beginning of whose end was so gruesomely ignoble. What is amazing is the myth of its irresistible strength which is dying so hard.

Considered historically, Russia's influence in Europe seems the most baseless thing in the world; a sort of convention invented by diplomatists for some dark purpose of their own, one would suspect, if the lack of grasp upon the realities of any given situation were not the main characteristic of the management of international relations. A glance back at the last hundred years shows the invariable, one may say the logical, powerlessness of Russia. As a military power it has never achieved by itself a single great thing. It has been indeed able to repel an ill-considered invasion, but only by having recourse to the extreme methods of desperation. In its attacks upon its specially selected victim this giant always struck as if with a withered right hand. All the campaigns against Turkey prove this, from Potemkin's time to the last Eastern war in 1878, entered upon with every advantage of a well-nursed prestige and a carefully fostered fanaticism. Even the half- armed were always too much for the might of Russia, or, rather, of the Tsardom. It was victorious only against the practically disarmed, as, in regard to its ideal of territorial expansion, a glance at a map will prove sufficiently. As an ally, Russia has been always unprofitable, taking her share in the defeats rather than in the victories of her friends, but always pushing her own claims with the arrogance of an arbiter of military success. She has been unable to help to any purpose a single principle to hold its own, not even the principle of authority and legitimism which Nicholas the First had declared so haughtily to rest under his special protection; just as Nicholas the Second has tried to make the maintenance of peace on earth his own exclusive affair. And the first Nicholas was a good Russian; he held the belief in the sacredness of his realm with such an intensity of faith that he could not survive the first shock of doubt. Rightly envisaged, the Crimean war was the end of what remained of absolutism and legitimism in Europe. It threw the way open for the liberation of Italy. The war in Manchuria makes an end of absolutism in Russia, whoever has got to perish from the shock behind a rampart of dead ukases, manifestoes, and rescripts. In the space of fifty years the self-appointed Apostle of Absolutism and the self-appointed Apostle of Peace, the Augustus and the Augustulus of the *regime* that was wont to speak contemptuously to European Foreign Offices in the beautiful French phrases of Prince Gorchakov, have fallen victims, each after his kind, to their shadowy and dreadful familiar, to the phantom, part ghoul, part Djinn, part Old Man of the Sea, with beak and claws and a double head, looking greedily both east and west on the confines of two continents.

That nobody through all that time penetrated the true nature of the monster it is impossible to believe. But of the many who must have seen, all were either too modest, too cautious, perhaps too discreet, to speak; or else were too insignificant to be heard or believed. Yet not all.

In the very early sixties, Prince Bismarck, then about to leave his post of Prussian Minister in St. Petersburg, called—so the story goes—upon another distinguished diplomatist. After some talk upon the general situation, the future Chancellor of the German Empire remarked that it was his practice to resume the impressions he had carried out of every country where he had made a long stay, in a short sentence, which he caused to be engraved upon some trinket. "I am leaving this country now, and this is what I bring away from it," he continued, taking off his finger a new ring to show to his colleague the inscription inside: "La Russie, c'est le neant."

Prince Bismarck had the truth of the matter and was neither too modest nor too discreet to speak out. Certainly he was not afraid of not being believed. Yet he did not shout his knowledge from the house-tops. He meant to have the phantom as his accomplice in an enterprise which has set the clock of peace back for many a year.

He had his way. The German Empire has been an accomplished fact for more than a third of a century—a great and dreadful legacy left to the world by the ill-omened phantom of Russia's might.

It is that phantom which is disappearing now—unexpectedly, astonishingly, as if by a touch of that wonderful magic for which the East has always been famous. The pretence of belief in its existence will no longer answer anybody's purposes (now Prince Bismarck is dead) unless the purposes of the writers of sensational paragraphs as to this *Neant* making an armed descent upon the plains of India. That sort of folly would be beneath notice if it did not distract attention from the real problem created for Europe by a war in the Far East.

For good or evil in the working out of her destiny, Russia is bound to remain a *Neant* for many long years, in a more even than a Bismarckian sense. The very fear of this spectre being gone, it behoves us to consider its legacy— the fact (no phantom that) accomplished in Central Europe by its help and connivance.

The German Empire may feel at bottom the loss of an old accomplice always amenable to the confidential whispers of a bargain; but in the first instance it cannot but rejoice at the fundamental weakening of a possible obstacle to its instincts of territorial expansion. There is a removal of that latent feeling of restraint which the presence of a powerful neighbour, however implicated with you in a sense of common guilt, is bound to inspire. The common guilt of the two Empires is defined precisely by their frontier line running through the Polish provinces. Without indulging in excessive feelings of indignation at that country's partition, or going so far as to believe—with a late French politician—in the "immanente justice des choses," it is clear that a material situation, based upon an essentially immoral transaction, contains the germ of fatal differences in the temperament of the two partners in iniquity— whatever the iniquity is. Germany has been the evil counsellor of Russia on all the questions of her Polish problem. Always urging the adoption of the most repressive measures with a perfectly logical duplicity, Prince Bismarck's Empire has taken care to couple the neighbourly offers of military assistance with merciless advice. The thought of the Polish provinces accepting a frank reconciliation with a humanised Russia and bringing the weight of homogeneous loyalty within a few miles of Berlin, has been always intensely distasteful to the arrogant Germanising tendencies of the other partner in iniquity. And, besides, the way to the Baltic provinces leads over the Niemen and over the Vistula.

And now, when there is a possibility of serious internal disturbances destroying the sort of order autocracy has kept in Russia, the road over these rivers is seen wearing a more inviting aspect. At any moment the pretext of armed intervention may be found in a revolutionary outbreak provoked by Socialists, perhaps—but at any rate by the political immaturity of the enlightened classes and by the political barbarism of the Russian people. The throes of Russian resurrection will be long and painful. This is not the place to speculate upon the nature of these convulsions, but there must be some violent break-up of the lamentable tradition, a shattering of the social, of the administrative— certainly of the territorial—unity.

Voices have been heard saying that the time for reforms in Russia is already past. This is the superficial view of the more profound truth that for Russia there has never been such a time within the memory of mankind. It is impossible to initiate a rational scheme of reform upon a phase of blind absolutism; and in Russia there has never been anything else to which the faintest tradition could, after ages of error, go back as to a parting of ways.

In Europe the old monarchical principle stands justified in its historical struggle with the growth of political liberty by the evolution of the idea of nationality as we see it concreted at the present time; by the inception of that wider solidarity grouping together around the standard of monarchical power these larger, agglomerations of mankind. This service of unification, creating close-knit communities possessing the ability, the will, and the power to pursue a common ideal, has prepared the ground for the advent of a still larger understanding: for the solidarity of Europeanism, which must be the next step towards the advent of Concord and Justice; an advent that, however delayed by the fatal worship of force and the errors of national selfishness, has been, and remains, the only possible goal of our progress.

The conceptions of legality, of larger patriotism, of national duties and aspirations have grown under the shadow of the old monarchies of Europe, which were the creations of historical necessity. There were seeds of wisdom in their very mistakes and abuses. They had a past and a future; they were human. But under the shadow of Russian autocracy nothing could grow. Russian autocracy succeeded to nothing; it had no historical past, and it cannot hope for a historical future. It can only end. By no industry of investigation, by no fantastic stretch of benevolence, can it be presented as a phase of development through which a Society, a State, must pass on the way to the full consciousness of its destiny. It lies outside the stream of progress. This despotism has been utterly un-European. Neither has it been Asiatic in its nature. Oriental despotisms belong to the history of mankind; they have left their trace on our minds and our imagination by their splendour, by their culture, by their art, by the exploits of great conquerors. The record of their rise and decay has an intellectual value; they are in their origins and their course the manifestations of human needs, the instruments of racial temperament, of catastrophic force, of faith and fanaticism. The Russian autocracy as we see it now is a thing apart. It is impossible to assign to it any rational origin in the vices, the misfortunes, the necessities, or the aspirations of mankind. That despotism has neither an European nor an Oriental parentage; more, it seems to have no root either in the institutions or the follies of this earth. What strikes one with a sort of awe is just this something inhuman in its character. It is like a visitation, like a curse from Heaven falling in the darkness of ages upon the immense plains of forest and steppe lying dumbly on the confines of two continents: a true desert harbouring no Spirit either of the East or of the West.

This pitiful fate of a country held by an evil spell, suffering from an awful visitation for which the responsibility cannot be traced either to her sins or her follies, has made Russia as a nation so difficult to understand by Europe. From the very first ghastly dawn of her existence as a State she had to breathe the atmosphere of despotism; she found nothing but the arbitrary will of an obscure autocrat at the beginning and end of her organisation. Hence arises her impenetrability to whatever is true in Western thought. Western thought, when it crosses her frontier, falls under the spell of her autocracy and becomes a noxious parody of itself. Hence the contradictions, the riddles of her national life, which are looked upon with such curiosity by the rest of the world. The curse had entered her very soul; autocracy, and nothing else in the world, has moulded her institutions, and with the poison of slavery drugged the national temperament into the apathy of a hopeless fatalism. It seems to have gone into the blood, tainting every mental activity in its source by a half-mystical, insensate, fascinating assertion of purity and holiness. The Government of Holy Russia, arrogating to itself the supreme power to torment and slaughter the bodies of its subjects like a God-sent scourge, has been most cruel to those whom it allowed to live under the shadow of its dispensation. The worst crime against humanity of that system we behold now crouching at bay behind vast heaps of mangled corpses is the ruthless destruction of innumerable minds. The greatest horror of the world—madness—walked faithfully in its train. Some of the best intellects of Russia, after struggling in vain against the spell, ended by throwing themselves at the feet of that hopeless despotism as a giddy man leaps into an abyss. An attentive survey of Russia's literature, of her Church, of her administration and the cross-currents of her thought, must end in the verdict that the Russia of to-day has not the right to give her voice on a single question touching the future of humanity, because from the very inception of her being the brutal destruction of dignity, of truth, of rectitude, of all that is faithful in human nature has been made the imperative condition of her existence. The great governmental secret of that imperium which Prince Bismarck had the insight and the courage to call *Le Neant*, has been the extirpation of every intellectual hope. To pronounce in the face of such a past the word Evolution, which is precisely the expression of the highest intellectual hope, is a gruesome pleasantry. There can be no evolution out of a grave. Another word of less scientific sound has been very much pronounced of late in connection with Russia's future, a word of more vague import, a word of dread as much as of hope—Revolution.

In the face of the events of the last four months, this word has sprung instinctively, as it were, on grave lips, and has been heard with solemn forebodings. More or less consciously, Europe is preparing herself for a spectacle of much violence and perhaps of an inspiring nobility of greatness. And there will be nothing of what she expects. She will see neither the anticipated character of the violence, nor yet any signs of generous greatness. Her expectations, more or less vaguely expressed, give the measure of her ignorance of that *Neant* which for so many years had remained hidden behind this phantom of invincible armies.

Neant! In a way, yes! And yet perhaps Prince Bismarck has let himself be led away by the seduction of a good phrase into the use of an inexact form. The form of his judgment had to be pithy, striking, engraved within a ring. If he erred, then, no doubt, he erred deliberately. The saying was near enough the truth to serve, and perhaps he did not want to destroy utterly by a more severe definition the prestige of the sham that could not deceive his genius. Prince Bismarck has been really complimentary to the useful phantom of the autocratic might. There is an awe-inspiring idea of infinity conveyed in the word *Neant*— and in Russia there is no idea. She is not a *Neant*, she is and has been simply the negation of everything worth living for. She is not an empty void, she is a yawning chasm open between East and West; a bottomless abyss that has swallowed up every hope of mercy, every aspiration towards personal dignity, towards freedom, towards knowledge, every ennobling desire of the heart, every redeeming whisper of conscience. Those that have peered into that abyss, where the dreams of Panslavism, of universal conquest, mingled with the hate and contempt for Western ideas, drift impotently like shapes of mist, know well that it is bottomless; that there is in it no ground for anything that could in the remotest degree serve even the lowest interests of mankind—and certainly no ground ready for a revolution. The sin of the old European monarchies was not the absolutism inherent in every form of government; it was the inability to alter the forms of their legality, grown narrow and oppressive with the march of time. Every form of legality is bound to degenerate into oppression, and the legality in the forms of monarchical institutions sooner, perhaps, than any other. It has not been the business of monarchies to be adaptive from within. With the mission of uniting and consolidating the particular ambitions and interests of feudalism in favour of a larger conception of a State, of giving self-consciousness, force and nationality to the scattered energies of thought and action, they were fated to lag behind the march of ideas they had themselves set in motion in a direction they could neither understand nor approve. Yet, for all that, the thrones still remain, and what is more significant, perhaps, some of the dynasties, too, have survived. The revolutions of European States have never been in the nature of absolute protests *en masse* against the monarchical principle; they were the uprising of the people against the oppressive degeneration of legality. But there never has been any legality in Russia; she is a negation of that as of everything else that has its root in reason or conscience. The ground of every revolution had to be intellectually prepared. A revolution is a short cut in the rational development of national needs in response to the growth of world-wide ideals. It is conceivably possible for a monarch of genius to put himself at the head of a revolution without ceasing to be the king of his people. For the autocracy of Holy Russia the only conceivable self-reform is—suicide.

The same relentless fate holds in its grip the all-powerful ruler and his helpless people. Wielders of a power purchased by an unspeakable baseness of subjection to the Khans of the Tartar horde, the Princes of Russia who, in their heart of hearts had come in time to regard themselves as superior to every monarch of Europe, have never risen to be the chiefs of a nation. Their authority has never been sanctioned by popular tradition, by ideas of intelligent loyalty, of devotion, of political necessity, of simple expediency, or even by the power of the sword. In whatever form of upheaval autocratic Russia is to find her end, it can never be a revolution fruitful of moral consequences to mankind. It cannot be anything else but a rising of slaves. It is a tragic circumstance that the only thing one can wish to that people who had never seen face to face either law, order, justice, right, truth about itself or the rest of the world; who had known nothing outside the capricious will of its irresponsible masters, is that it should find in the approaching hour of need, not an organiser or a law-giver, with the wisdom of a Lycurgus or a Solon for their service, but at least the force of energy and desperation in some as yet unknown Spartacus.

A brand of hopeless mental and moral inferiority is set upon Russian achievements; and the coming events of her internal changes, however appalling they may be in their magnitude, will be nothing more impressive than the convulsions of a colossal body. As her boasted military force that, corrupt in its origin, has ever struck no other but faltering blows, so her soul, kept benumbed by her temporal and spiritual master with the poison of tyranny and superstition, will find itself on awakening possessed of no language, a monstrous full-grown child having first to learn the ways of living thought and articulate speech. It is safe to say tyranny, assuming a thousand protean shapes, will remain clinging to her struggles for a long time before her blind multitudes succeed at last in trampling her out of existence under their millions of bare feet.

That would be the beginning. What is to come after? The conquest of freedom to call your soul your own is only the first step on the road to excellence. We, in Europe, have gone a step or two further, have had the time to forget how little that freedom means. To Russia it must seem everything. A prisoner shut up in a noisome dungeon concentrates all his hope and desire on the moment of stepping out beyond the gates. It appears to him pregnant with an immense and final importance; whereas what is important is the spirit in which he will draw the first breath of freedom, the counsels he will hear, the hands he may find extended, the endless days of toil that must follow, wherein he will have to build his future with no other material but what he can find within himself.

It would be vain for Russia to hope for the support and counsel of collective wisdom. Since 1870 (as a distinguished statesman of the old tradition disconsolately exclaimed) "il n'y a plus d'Europe!" There is, indeed, no Europe. The idea of a Europe united in the solidarity of her dynasties, which for a moment seemed to dawn on the horizon of the Vienna Congress through the subsiding dust of Napoleonic alarums and excursions, has been extinguished by the larger glamour of less restraining ideals. Instead of the doctrines of solidarity it was the doctrine of nationalities much more favourable to spoliations that came to the front, and since its greatest triumphs at Sadowa and Sedan there is no Europe. Meanwhile till the time comes when there will be no frontiers, there are alliances so shamelessly based upon the exigencies of suspicion and mistrust that their cohesive force waxes and wanes with every year, almost with the event of every passing month. This is the atmosphere Russia will find when the last rampart of tyranny has been beaten down. But what hands, what voices will she find on coming out into the light of day? An ally she has yet who more than any other of Russia's allies has found that it had parted with lots of solid substance in exchange for a shadow. It is true that the shadow was indeed the mightiest, the darkest that the modern world had ever known—and the most overbearing. But it is fading now, and the tone of truest anxiety as to what is to take its place will come, no doubt, from that and no other direction, and no doubt, also, it will have that note of generosity which even in the moments of greatest aberration is seldom wanting in the voice of the French people.

Two neighbours Russia will find at her door. Austria, traditionally unaggressive whenever her hand is not forced, ruled by a dynasty of uncertain future, weakened by her duality, can only speak to her in an uncertain, bilingual phrase. Prussia, grown in something like forty years from an almost pitiful dependant into a bullying friend and evil counsellor of Russia's masters, may, indeed, hasten to extend a strong hand to the weakness of her exhausted body, but if so it will be only with the intention of tearing away the long-coveted part of her substance.

Pan-Germanism is by no means a shape of mists, and Germany is anything but a *Néant* where thought and effort are likely to lose themselves without sound or trace. It is a powerful and voracious organisation, full of unscrupulous self-confidence, whose appetite for aggrandisement will only be limited by the power of helping itself to the severed members of its friends and neighbours. The era of wars so eloquently denounced by the old Republicans as the peculiar blood guilt of dynastic ambitions is by no means over yet. They will be fought out differently, with lesser frequency, with an increased bitterness and the savage tooth- and-claw obstinacy of a struggle for existence. They will make us regret the time of dynastic ambitions, with their human absurdity moderated by prudence and even by shame, by the fear of personal responsibility and the regard paid to certain forms of conventional decency. For, if the monarchs of Europe have been derided for addressing each other as "brother" in autograph communications, that relationship was at least as effective as any form of brotherhood likely to be established between the rival nations of this continent, which, we are assured on all hands, is the heritage of democracy. In the ceremonial brotherhood of monarchs the reality of blood-ties, for what little it is worth, acted often as a drag on unscrupulous desires of glory or greed. Besides, there was always the common danger of exasperated peoples, and some respect for each other's divine right. No leader of a democracy, without other ancestry but the sudden shout of a multitude, and debarred by the very condition of his power from even thinking of a direct heir, will have any interest in calling brother the leader of another democracy—a chief as fatherless and heirless as himself.

The war of 1870, brought about by the third Napoleon's half-generous, half-selfish adoption of the principle of nationalities, was the first war characterised by a special intensity of hate, by a new note in the tune of an old song for which we may thank the Teutonic thoroughness. Was it not that excellent bourgeoise, Princess Bismarck (to keep only to great examples), who was so righteously anxious to see men, women and children—emphatically the children, too—of the abominable French nation massacred off the face of the earth? This illustration of the new war- temper is artlessly revealed in the prattle of the amiable Busch, the Chancellor's pet "reptile" of the Press. And this was supposed to be a war for an idea! Too much, however, should not be made of that good wife's and mother's sentiments any more than of the good First Emperor William's tears, shed so abundantly after every battle, by letter, telegram, and otherwise, during the course of the same war, before a dumb and shamefaced continent. These were merely the expressions of the simplicity of a nation which more than any other has a tendency to run into the grotesque. There is worse to come.

To-day, in the fierce grapple of two nations of different race, the short era of national wars seems about to close. No war will be waged for an idea. The "noxious idle aristocracies" of yesterday fought without malice for an occupation, for the honour, for the fun of the thing. The virtuous, industrious democratic States of to-morrow may yet be reduced to fighting for a crust of dry bread, with all the hate, ferocity, and fury that must attach to the vital importance of such an issue. The dreams sanguine humanitarians raised almost to ecstasy about the year fifty of the last century by the moving sight of the Crystal Palace—crammed full with that variegated rubbish which it seems to be the bizarre fate of humanity to produce for the benefit of a few employers of labour—have vanished as quickly as they had arisen. The golden hopes of peace have in a single night turned to dead leaves in every drawer of every benevolent theorist's writing table. A swift disenchantment overtook the incredible infatuation which could put its trust in the peaceful nature of industrial and commercial competition.

Industrialism and commercialism—wearing high-sounding names in many languages (*Welt-politik* may serve for one instance) picking up coins behind the severe and disdainful figure of science whose giant strides have widened for us the horizon of the universe by some few inches—stand ready, almost eager, to appeal to the sword as soon as the globe of the earth has shrunk beneath our growing numbers by another ell or so. And democracy, which has elected to pin its faith to the supremacy of material interests, will have to fight their battles to the bitter end, on a mere pittance—unless, indeed, some statesman of exceptional ability and overwhelming prestige succeeds in carrying through an international understanding for the delimitation of spheres of trade all over the earth, on the model of the territorial spheres of influence marked in Africa to keep the competitors for the privilege of improving the nigger (as a buying machine) from flying prematurely at each other's throats.

This seems the only expedient at hand for the temporary maintenance of European peace, with its alliances based on mutual distrust, preparedness for war as its ideal, and the fear of wounds, luckily stronger, so far, than the pinch of hunger, its only guarantee. The true peace of the world will be a place of refuge much less like a beleaguered fortress and more, let us hope, in the nature of an Inviolable Temple. It will be built on less perishable foundations than those of material interests. But it must be confessed that the architectural aspect of the universal city remains as yet inconceivable—that the very ground for its erection has not been cleared of the jungle.

Never before in history has the right of war been more fully admitted in the rounded periods of public speeches, in books, in public prints, in all the public works of peace, culminating in the establishment of the Hague Tribunal—that solemnly official recognition of the Earth as a House of Strife. To him whose indignation is qualified by a measure of hope and affection, the efforts of mankind to work its own salvation present a sight of alarming comicality. After clinging for ages to the steps of the heavenly throne, they are now, without much modifying their attitude, trying with touching ingenuity to steal one by one the thunderbolts of their Jupiter. They have removed war from the list of Heaven-sent visitations that could only be prayed against; they have erased its name from the supplication against the wrath of war, pestilence, and famine, as it is found in the litanies of the Roman Catholic Church; they have dragged the scourge down from the skies and have made it into a calm and regulated institution. At first sight the change does not seem for the better. Jove's thunderbolt looks a most dangerous plaything in the hands of the people. But a solemnly established institution begins to grow old at once in the discussion, abuse, worship, and execration of men. It grows obsolete, odious, and intolerable; it stands fatally condemned to an unhonoured old age.

Therein lies the best hope of advanced thought, and the best way to help its prospects is to provide in the fullest, frankest way for the conditions of the present day. War is one of its conditions; it is its principal condition. It lies at the heart of every question agitating the fears and hopes of a humanity divided against itself. The succeeding ages have changed nothing except the watchwords of the armies. The intellectual stage of mankind being as yet in its infancy, and States, like most individuals, having but a feeble and imperfect consciousness of the worth and force of the inner life, the need of making their existence manifest to themselves is determined in the direction of physical activity. The idea of ceasing to grow in territory, in strength, in wealth, in influence—in anything but wisdom and self-knowledge—is odious to them as the omen of the end. Action, in which is to be found the illusion of a mastered destiny, can alone satisfy our uneasy vanity and lay to rest the haunting fear of the future—a sentiment concealed, indeed, but proving its existence by the force it has, when invoked, to stir the passions of a nation. It will be long before we have learned that in the great darkness before us there is nothing that we need fear. Let us act lest we perish—is the cry. And the only form of action open to a State can be of no other than aggressive nature.

There are many kinds of aggressions, though the sanction of them is one and the same—the magazine rifle of the latest pattern. In preparation for or against that form of action the States of Europe are spending now such moments of uneasy leisure as they can snatch from the labours of factory and counting-house.

Never before has war received so much homage at the lips of men, and reigned with less disputed sway in their minds. It has harnessed science to its gun-carriages, it has enriched a few respectable manufacturers, scattered doles of food and raiment amongst a few thousand skilled workmen, devoured the first youth of whole generations, and reaped its harvest of countless corpses. It has perverted the intelligence of men, women, and children, and has made the speeches of Emperors, Kings, Presidents, and Ministers monotonous with ardent protestations of fidelity to peace. Indeed, war has made peace altogether its own, it has modelled it on its own image: a martial, overbearing, war-lord sort of peace, with a mailed fist, and turned-up moustaches, ringing with the din of grand manoeuvres, eloquent with allusions to glorious feats of arms; it has made peace so magnificent as to be almost as expensive to keep up as itself. It has sent out apostles of its own, who at one time went about (mostly in newspapers) preaching the gospel of the mystic sanctity of its sacrifices, and the regenerating power of spilt blood, to the poor in mind—whose name is legion.

It has been observed that in the course of earthly greatness a day of culminating triumph is often paid for by a morrow of sudden extinction. Let us hope it is so. Yet the dawn of that day of retribution may be a long time breaking above a dark horizon. War is with us now; and, whether this one ends soon or late, war will be with us again. And it is the way of true wisdom for men and States to take account of things as they are.

Civilisation has done its little best by our sensibilities for whose growth it is responsible. It has managed to remove the sights and sounds of battlefields away from our doorsteps. But it cannot be expected to achieve the feat always and under every variety of circumstance. Some day it must fail, and we shall have then a wealth of appallingly unpleasant sensations brought home to us with painful intimacy. It is not absurd to suppose that whatever war comes to us next it will *not* be a distant war waged by Russia either beyond the Amur or beyond the Oxus.

The Japanese armies have laid that ghost for ever, because the Russia of the future will not, for the reasons explained above, be the Russia of to-day. It will not have the same thoughts, resentments and aims. It is even a question whether it will preserve its gigantic frame unaltered and unbroken. All speculation loses itself in the magnitude of the events made possible by the defeat of an autocracy whose only shadow of a title to existence was the invincible power of military conquest. That autocratic Russia will have a miserable end in harmony with its base origin and inglorious life does not seem open to doubt. The problem of the immediate future is posed not by the eventual manner but by the approaching fact of its disappearance.

The Japanese armies, in laying the oppressive ghost, have not only accomplished what will be recognised historically as an important mission in the world's struggle against all forms of evil, but have also created a situation. They have created a situation in the East which they are competent to manage by themselves; and in doing this they have brought about a change in the condition of the West with which Europe is not well prepared to deal. The common ground of concord, good faith and justice is not sufficient to establish an action upon; since the conscience of but very few men amongst us, and of no single Western nation as yet, will brook the restraint of abstract ideas as against the fascination of a material advantage. And eagle-eyed wisdom alone cannot take the lead of human action, which in its nature must for ever remain short-sighted. The trouble of the civilised world is the want of a common conservative principle abstract enough to give the impulse, practical enough to form the rallying point of international action tending towards the restraint of particular ambitions. Peace tribunals instituted for the greater glory of war will not replace it. Whether such a principle exists—who can say? If it does not, then it ought to be invented. A sage with a sense of humour and a heart of compassion should set about it without loss of time, and a solemn prophet full of words and fire ought to be given the task of preparing the minds. So far there is no trace of such a principle anywhere in sight; even its plausible imitations (never very effective) have disappeared long ago before the doctrine of national aspirations. *Il n'y a plus d'Europe*—there is only an armed and trading continent, the home of slowly maturing economical contests for life and death and of loudly proclaimed world-wide ambitions. There are also other ambitions not so loud, but deeply rooted in the envious acquisitive temperament of the last corner amongst the great Powers of the Continent, whose feet are not exactly in the ocean—not yet—and whose head is very high up—in Pomerania, the breeding place of such precious Grenadiers that Prince Bismarck (whom it is a pleasure to quote) would not have given the bones of one of them for the settlement of the old Eastern Question. But times have changed, since, by way of keeping up, I suppose, some old barbaric German rite, the faithful servant of the Hohenzollerns was buried alive to celebrate the accession of a new Emperor.

Already the voice of surmises has been heard hinting tentatively at a possible re-grouping of European Powers. The alliance of the three Empires is supposed possible. And it may be possible. The myth of Russia's power is dying very hard—hard enough for that combination to take place—such is the fascination that a discredited show of numbers will still exercise upon the imagination of a people trained to the worship of force. Germany may be willing to lend its support to a tottering autocracy for the sake of an undisputed first place, and of a preponderating voice in the settlement of every question in that south- east of Europe which merges into Asia. No principle being involved in such an alliance of mere expediency, it would never be allowed to stand in the way of Germany's other ambitions. The fall of autocracy would bring its restraint automatically to an end. Thus it may be believed that the support Russian despotism may get from its once humble friend and client will not be stamped by that thoroughness which is supposed to be the mark of German superiority. Russia weakened down to the second place, or Russia eclipsed altogether during the throes of her regeneration, will answer equally well the plans of German policy—which are many and various and often incredible, though the aim of them all is the same: aggrandisement of territory and influence, with no regard to right and justice, either in the East or in the West. For that and no other is the true note of your *Welt-politik* which desires to live.

The German eagle with a Prussian head looks all round the horizon, not so much for something to do that would count for good in the records of the earth, as simply for something good to get. He gazes upon the land and upon the sea with the same covetous steadiness, for he has become of late a maritime eagle, and has learned to box the compass. He gazes north and south, and east and west, and is inclined to look intemperately upon the waters of the Mediterranean when they are blue. The disappearance of the Russian phantom has given a foreboding of unwonted freedom to the *Welt- politik*. According to the national tendency this assumption of Imperial impulses would run into the grotesque were it not for the spikes of the *pickelhaubes* peeping out grimly from behind. Germany's attitude proves that no peace for the earth can be found in the expansion of material interests which she seems to have adopted exclusively as her only aim, ideal, and watchword. For the use of those who gaze half-unbelieving at the passing away of the Russian phantom, part Ghoul, part Djinn, part Old Man of the Sea, and wait half-doubting for the birth of a nation's soul in this age which knows no miracles, the once-famous saying of poor Gambetta, tribune of the people (who was simple and believed in the "immanent justice of things"), may be adapted in the shape of a warning that, so far as a future of liberty, concord, and justice is concerned: "Le Prussianisme—voila l'ennemi!"

THE CRIME OF PARTITION—1919

At the end of the eighteenth century, when the partition of Poland had become an accomplished fact, the world qualified it at once as a crime. This strong condemnation proceeded, of course, from the West of Europe; the Powers of the Centre, Prussia and Austria, were not likely to admit that this spoliation fell into the category of acts morally reprehensible and carrying the taint of anti-social guilt. As to Russia, the third party to the crime, and the originator of the scheme, she had no national conscience at the time. The will of its rulers was always accepted by the people as the expression of an omnipotence derived directly from God. As an act of mere conquest the best excuse for the partition lay simply in the fact that it happened to be possible; there was the plunder and there was the opportunity to get hold of it. Catherine the Great looked upon this extension of her dominions with a cynical satisfaction. Her political argument that the destruction of Poland meant the repression of revolutionary ideas and the checking of the spread of Jacobinism in Europe was a characteristically impudent pretence. There may have been minds here and there amongst the Russians that perceived, or perhaps only felt, that by the annexation of the greater part of the Polish Republic, Russia approached nearer to the comity of civilised nations and ceased, at least territorially, to be an Asiatic Power.

It was only after the partition of Poland that Russia began to play a great part in Europe. To such statesmen as she had then that act of brigandage must have appeared inspired by great political wisdom. The King of Prussia, faithful to the ruling principle of his life, wished simply to aggrandise his dominions at a much smaller cost and at much less risk than he could have done in any other direction; for at that time Poland was perfectly defenceless from a material point of view, and more than ever, perhaps, inclined to put its faith in humanitarian illusions. Morally, the Republic was in a state of ferment and consequent weakness, which so often accompanies the period of social reform. The strength arrayed against her was just then overwhelming; I mean the comparatively honest (because open) strength of armed forces. But, probably from innate inclination towards treachery, Frederick of Prussia selected for himself the part of falsehood and deception. Appearing on the scene in the character of a friend he entered deliberately into a treaty of alliance with the Republic, and then, before the ink was dry, tore it up in brazen defiance of the commonest decency, which must have been extremely gratifying to his natural tastes.

As to Austria, it shed diplomatic tears over the transaction. They cannot be called crocodile tears, insomuch that they were in a measure sincere. They arose from a vivid perception that Austria's allotted share of the spoil could never compensate her for the accession of strength and territory to the other two Powers. Austria did not really want an extension of territory at the cost of Poland. She could not hope to improve her frontier in that way, and economically she had no need of Galicia, a province whose natural resources were undeveloped and whose salt mines did not arouse her cupidity because she had salt mines of her own. No doubt the democratic complexion of Polish institutions was very distasteful to the conservative monarchy; Austrian statesmen did see at the time that the real danger to the principle of autocracy was in the West, in France, and that all the forces of Central Europe would be needed for its suppression. But the movement towards a *partage* on the part of Russia and Prussia was too definite to be resisted, and Austria had to follow their lead in the destruction of a State which she would have preferred to preserve as a possible ally against Prussian and Russian ambitions. It may be truly said that the destruction of Poland secured the safety of the French Revolution. For when in 1795 the crime was consummated, the Revolution had turned the corner and was in a state to defend itself against the forces of reaction.

In the second half of the eighteenth century there were two centres of liberal ideas on the continent of Europe: France and Poland. On an impartial survey one may say without exaggeration that then France was relatively every bit as weak as Poland; even, perhaps, more so. But France's geographical position made her much less vulnerable. She had no powerful neighbours on her frontier; a decayed Spain in the south and a conglomeration of small German Principalities on the east were her happy lot. The only States which dreaded the contamination of the new principles and had enough power to combat it were Prussia, Austria, and Russia, and they had another centre of forbidden ideas to deal with in defenceless Poland, unprotected by nature, and offering an immediate satisfaction to their cupidity. They made their choice, and the untold sufferings of a nation which would not die was the price exacted by fate for the triumph of revolutionary ideals.

Thus even a crime may become a moral agent by the lapse of time and the course of history. Progress leaves its dead by the way, for progress is only a great adventure as its leaders and chiefs know very well in their hearts. It is a march into an undiscovered country; and in such an enterprise the victims do not count. As an emotional outlet for the oratory of freedom it was convenient enough to remember the Crime now and then: the Crime being the murder of a State and the carving of its body into three pieces. There was really nothing to do but to drop a few tears and a few flowers of rhetoric upon the grave. But the spirit of the nation refused to rest therein. It haunted the territories of the Old Republic in the manner of a ghost haunting its ancestral mansion where strangers are making themselves at home; a calumniated, ridiculed, and pooh-pooh'd ghost, and yet never ceasing to inspire a sort of awe, a strange uneasiness, in the hearts of the unlawful possessors. Poland deprived of its independence, of its historical continuity, with its religion and language persecuted and repressed, became a mere geographical expression. And even that, itself, seemed strangely vague, had lost its definite character, was rendered doubtful by the theories and the claims of the spoliators who, by a strange effect of uneasy conscience, while strenuously denying the moral guilt of the transaction, were always trying to throw a veil of high rectitude over the Crime. What was most annoying to their righteousness was the fact that the nation, stabbed to the heart, refused to grow insensible and cold. That persistent and almost uncanny vitality was sometimes very inconvenient to the rest of Europe also. It would intrude its irresistible claim into every problem of European politics, into the theory of European equilibrium, into the question of the Near East, the Italian question, the question of Schleswig-Holstein, and into the doctrine of nationalities. That ghost, not content with making its ancestral halls uncomfortable for the thieves, haunted also the Cabinets of Europe, waved indecently its bloodstained robes in the solemn atmosphere of Council- rooms, where congresses and conferences sit with closed windows. It would not be exorcised by the brutal jeers of Bismarck and the fine railleries of Gorchakov.

As a Polish friend observed to me some years ago: "Till the year '48 the Polish problem has been to a certain extent a convenient rallying-point for all manifestations of liberalism. Since that time we have come to be regarded simply as a nuisance. It's very disagreeable."

I agreed that it was, and he continued: "What are we to do? We did not create the situation by any outside action of ours. Through all the centuries of its existence Poland has never been a menace to anybody, not even to the Turks, to whom it has been merely an obstacle."

Nothing could be more true. The spirit of aggressiveness was absolutely foreign to the Polish temperament, to which the preservation of its institutions and its liberties was much more precious than any ideas of conquest. Polish wars were defensive, and they were mostly fought within Poland's own borders. And that those territories were often invaded was but a misfortune arising from its geographical position. Territorial expansion was never the master-thought of Polish statesmen. The consolidation of the territories of the *serenissime* Republic, which made of it a Power of the first rank for a time, was not accomplished by force. It was not the consequence of successful aggression, but of a long and successful defence against the raiding neighbours from the East. The lands of Lithuanian and Ruthenian speech were never conquered by Poland. These peoples were not compelled by a series of exhausting wars to seek safety in annexation. It was not the will of a prince or a political intrigue that brought about the union. Neither was it fear. The slowly-matured view of the economical and social necessities and, before all, the ripening moral sense of the masses were the motives that induced the forty three representatives of Lithuanian and Ruthenian provinces, led by their paramount prince, to enter into a political combination unique in the history of the world, a spontaneous and complete union of sovereign States choosing deliberately the way of peace. Never was strict truth better expressed in a political instrument than in the preamble of the first Union Treaty (1413). It begins with the words: "This Union, being the outcome not of hatred, but of love"—words that Poles have not heard addressed to them politically by any nation for the last hundred and fifty years.

This union being an organic, living thing capable of growth and development was, later, modified and confirmed by two other treaties, which guaranteed to all the parties in a just and eternal union all their rights, liberties, and respective institutions. The Polish State offers a singular instance of an extremely liberal administrative federalism which, in its Parliamentary life as well as its international politics, presented a complete unity of feeling and purpose. As an eminent French diplomatist remarked many years ago: "It is a very remarkable fact in the history of the Polish State, this invariable and unanimous consent of the populations; the more so that, the King being looked upon simply as the chief of the Republic, there was no monarchical bond, no dynastic fidelity to control and guide the sentiment of the nations, and their union remained as a pure affirmation of the national will." The Grand Duchy of Lithuania and its Ruthenian Provinces retained their statutes, their own administration, and their own political institutions. That those institutions in the course of time tended to assimilation with the Polish form was not the result of any pressure, but simply of the superior character of Polish civilisation.

Even after Poland lost its independence this alliance and this union remained firm in spirit and fidelity. All the national movements towards liberation were initiated in the name of the whole mass of people inhabiting the limits of the old Republic, and all the Provinces took part in them with complete devotion. It is only in the last generation that efforts have been made to create a tendency towards separation, which would indeed serve no one but Poland's common enemies. And, strangely enough, it is the internationalists, men who professedly care nothing for race or country, who have set themselves this task of disruption, one can easily see for what sinister purpose. The ways of the internationalists may be dark, but they are not inscrutable.

From the same source no doubt there will flow in the future a poisoned stream of hints of a reconstituted Poland being a danger to the races once so closely associated within the territories of the Old Republic. The old partners in "the Crime" are not likely to forgive their victim its inconvenient and almost shocking obstinacy in keeping alive. They had tried moral assassination before and with some small measure of success, for, indeed, the Polish question, like all living reproaches, had become a nuisance. Given the wrong, and the apparent impossibility of righting it without running risks of a serious nature, some moral alleviation may be found in the belief that the victim had brought its misfortunes on its own head by its own sins. That theory, too, had been advanced about Poland (as if other nations had known nothing of sin and folly), and it made some way in the world at different times, simply because good care was taken by the interested parties to stop the mouth of the accused. But it has never carried much conviction to honest minds. Somehow, in defiance of the cynical point of view as to the Force of Lies and against all the power of falsified evidence, truth often turns out to be stronger than calumny. With the course of years, however, another danger sprang up, a danger arising naturally from the new political alliances dividing Europe into two armed camps. It was the danger of silence. Almost without exception the Press of Western Europe in the twentieth century refused to touch the Polish question in any shape or form whatever. Never was the fact of Polish vitality more embarrassing to European diplomacy than on the eve of Poland's resurrection.

When the war broke out there was something gruesomely comic in the proclamations of emperors and archdukes appealing to that invincible soul of a nation whose existence or moral worth they had been so arrogantly denying for more than a century. Perhaps in the whole record of human transactions there have never been performances so brazen and so vile as the manifestoes of the German Emperor and the Grand Duke Nicholas of Russia; and, I imagine, no more bitter insult has been offered to human heart and intelligence than the way in which those proclamations were flung into the face of historical truth. It was like a scene in a cynical and sinister farce, the absurdity of which became in some sort unfathomable by the reflection that nobody in the world could possibly be so abjectly stupid as to be deceived for a single moment. At that time, and for the first two months of the war, I happened to be in Poland, and I remember perfectly well that, when those precious documents came out, the confidence in the moral turpitude of mankind they implied did not even raise a scornful smile on the lips of men whose most sacred feelings and dignity they outraged. They did not deign to waste their contempt on them. In fact, the situation was too poignant and too involved for either hot scorn or a coldly rational discussion. For the Poles it was like being in a burning house of which all the issues were locked. There was nothing but sheer anguish under the strange, as if stony, calmness which in the utter absence of all hope falls on minds that are not constitutionally prone to despair. Yet in this time of dismay the irrepressible vitality of the nation would not accept a neutral attitude. I was told that even if there were no issue it was absolutely necessary for the Poles to affirm their national existence. Passivity, which could be regarded as a craven acceptance of all the material and moral horrors ready to fall upon the nation, was not to be thought of for a moment. Therefore, it was explained to me, the Poles *must* act. Whether this was a counsel of wisdom or not it is very difficult to say, but there are crises of the soul which are beyond the reach of wisdom. When there is apparently no issue visible to the eyes of reason, sentiment may yet find a way out, either towards salvation or to utter perdition, no one can tell—and the sentiment does not even ask the question. Being there as a stranger in that tense atmosphere, which was yet not unfamiliar to me, I was not very anxious to parade my wisdom, especially after it had been pointed out in answer to my cautious arguments that, if life has its values worth fighting for, death, too, has that in it which can make it worthy or unworthy.

Out of the mental and moral trouble into which the grouping of the Powers at the beginning of war had thrown the counsels of Poland there emerged at last the decision that the Polish Legions, a peace organisation in Galicia directed by Pilsudski (afterwards given the rank of General, and now apparently the Chief of the Government in Warsaw), should take the field against the Russians. In reality it did not matter against which partner in the "Crime" Polish resentment should be directed. There was little to choose between the methods of Russian barbarism, which were both crude and rotten, and the cultivated brutality tinged with contempt of Germany's superficial, grinding civilisation. There was nothing to choose between them. Both were hateful, and the direction of the Polish effort was naturally governed by Austria's tolerant attitude, which had connived for years at the semi-secret organisation of the Polish Legions. Besides, the material possibility pointed out the way. That Poland should have turned at first against the ally of Western Powers, to whose moral support she had been looking for so many years, is not a greater monstrosity than that alliance with Russia which had been entered into by England and France with rather less excuse and with a view to eventualities which could perhaps have been avoided by a firmer policy and by a greater resolution in the face of what plainly appeared unavoidable.

For let the truth be spoken. The action of Germany, however cruel, sanguinary, and faithless, was nothing in the nature of a stab in the dark. The Germanic Tribes had told the whole world in all possible tones carrying conviction, the gently persuasive, the coldly logical; in tones Hegelian, Nietzschean, warlike, pious, cynical, inspired, what they were going to do to the inferior races of the earth, so full of sin and all unworthiness. But with a strange similarity to the prophets of old (who were also great moralists and invokers of might) they seemed to be crying in a desert. Whatever might have been the secret searching of hearts, the Worthless Ones would not take heed. It must also be admitted that the conduct of the menaced Governments carried with it no suggestion of resistance. It was no doubt, the effect of neither courage nor fear, but of that prudence which causes the average man to stand very still in the presence of a savage dog. It was not a very politic attitude, and the more reprehensible in so far that it seemed to arise from the mistrust of their own people's fortitude. On simple matters of life and death a people is always better than its leaders, because a people cannot argue itself as a whole into a sophisticated state of mind out of deference for a mere doctrine or from an exaggerated sense of its own cleverness. I am speaking now of democracies whose chiefs resemble the tyrant of Syracuse in this, that their power is unlimited (for who can limit the will of a voting people?) and who always see the domestic sword hanging by a hair above their heads.

Perhaps a different attitude would have checked German self-confidence, and her overgrown militarism would have died from the excess of its own strength. What would have been then the moral state of Europe it is difficult to say. Some other excess would probably have taken its place, excess of theory, or excess of sentiment, or an excess of the sense of security leading to some other form of catastrophe; but it is certain that in that case the Polish question would not have taken a concrete form for ages. Perhaps it would never have taken form! In this world, where everything is transient, even the most reproachful ghosts end by vanishing out of old mansions, out of men's consciences. Progress of enlightenment, or decay of faith? In the years before the war the Polish ghost was becoming so thin that it was impossible to get for it the slightest mention in the papers. A young Pole coming to me from Paris was extremely indignant, but I, indulging in that detachment which is the product of greater age, longer experience, and a habit of meditation, refused to share that sentiment. He had gone begging for a word on Poland to many influential people, and they had one and all told him that they were going to do no such thing. They were all men of ideas and therefore might have been called idealists, but the notion most strongly anchored in their minds was the folly of touching a question which certainly had no merit of actuality and would have had the appalling effect of provoking the wrath of their old enemies and at the same time offending the sensibilities of their new friends. It was an unanswerable argument. I couldn't share my young friend's surprise and indignation. My practice of reflection had also convinced me that there is nothing on earth that turns quicker on its pivot than political idealism when touched by the breath of practical politics.

It would be good to remember that Polish independence as embodied in a Polish State is not the gift of any kind of journalism, neither is it the outcome even of some particularly benevolent idea or of any clearly apprehended sense of guilt. I am speaking of what I know when I say that the original and only formative idea in Europe was the idea of delivering the fate of Poland into the hands of Russian Tsarism. And, let us remember, it was assumed then to be a victorious Tsarism at that. It was an idea talked of openly, entertained seriously, presented as a benevolence, with a curious blindness to its grotesque and ghastly character. It was the idea of delivering the victim with a kindly smile and the confident assurance that "it would be all right" to a perfectly unrepentant assassin, who, after sawing furiously at its throat for a hundred years or so, was expected to make friends suddenly and kiss it on both cheeks in the mystic Russian fashion. It was a singularly nightmarish combination of international polity, and no whisper of any other would have been officially tolerated. Indeed, I do not think in the whole extent of Western Europe there was anybody who had the slightest mind to whisper on that subject. Those were the days of the dark future, when Benckendorf put down his name on the Committee for the Relief of Polish Populations driven by the Russian armies into the heart of Russia, when the Grand Duke Nicholas (the gentleman who advocated a St. Bartholomew's Night for the suppression of Russian liberalism) was displaying his "divine" (I have read the very word in an English newspaper of standing) strategy in the great retreat, where Mr. Iswolsky carried himself haughtily on the banks of the Seine; and it was beginning to dawn upon certain people there that he was a greater nuisance even than the Polish question.

But there is no use in talking about all that. Some clever person has said that it is always the unexpected that happens, and on a calm and dispassionate survey the world does appear mainly to one as a scene of miracles. Out of Germany's strength, in whose purpose so many people refused to believe, came Poland's opportunity, in which nobody could have been expected to believe. Out of Russia's collapse emerged that forbidden thing, the Polish independence, not as a vengeful figure, the retributive shadow of the crime, but as something much more solid and more difficult to get rid of—a political necessity and a moral solution. Directly it appeared its practical usefulness became undeniable, and also the fact that, for better or worse, it was impossible to get rid of it again except by the unthinkable way of another carving, of another partition, of another crime.

Therein lie the strength and the future of the thing so strictly forbidden no farther back than two years or so, of the Polish independence expressed in a Polish State. It comes into the world morally free, not in virtue of its sufferings, but in virtue of its miraculous rebirth and of its ancient claim for services rendered to Europe. Not a single one of the combatants of all the fronts of the world has died consciously for Poland's freedom. That supreme opportunity was denied even to Poland's own children. And it is just as well! Providence in its inscrutable way had been merciful, for had it been otherwise the load of gratitude would have been too great, the sense of obligation too crushing, the joy of deliverance too fearful for mortals, common sinners with the rest of mankind before the eye of the Most High. Those who died East and West, leaving so much anguish and so much pride behind them, died neither for the creation of States, nor for empty words, nor yet for the salvation of general ideas. They died neither for democracy, nor leagues, nor systems, nor yet for abstract justice, which is an unfathomable mystery. They died for something too deep for words, too mighty for the common standards by which reason measures the advantages of life and death, too sacred for the vain discourses that come and go on the lips of dreamers, fanatics, humanitarians, and statesmen. They died . . . .

Poland's independence springs up from that great immolation, but Poland's loyalty to Europe will not be rooted in anything so trenchant and burdensome as the sense of an immeasurable indebtedness, of that gratitude which in a worldly sense is sometimes called eternal, but which lies always at the mercy of weariness and is fatally condemned by the instability of human sentiments to end in negation. Polish loyalty will be rooted in something much more solid and enduring, in something that could never be called eternal, but which is, in fact, life-enduring. It will be rooted in the national temperament, which is about the only thing on earth that can be trusted. Men may deteriorate, they may improve too, but they don't change. Misfortune is a hard school which may either mature or spoil a national character, but it may be reasonably advanced that the long course of adversity of the most cruel kind has not injured the fundamental characteristics of the Polish nation which has proved its vitality against the most demoralising odds. The various phases of the Polish sense of self-preservation struggling amongst the menacing forces and the no less threatening chaos of the neighbouring Powers should be judged impartially. I suggest impartiality and not indulgence simply because, when appraising the Polish question, it is not necessary to invoke the softer emotions. A little calm reflection on the past and the present is all that is necessary on the part of the Western world to judge the movements of a community whose ideals are the same, but whose situation is unique. This situation was brought vividly home to me in the course of an argument more than eighteen months ago. "Don't forget," I was told, "that Poland has got to live in contact with Germany and Russia to the end of time. Do you understand the force of that expression: 'To the end of time'? Facts must be taken into account, and especially appalling facts, such as this, to which there is no possible remedy on earth. For reasons which are, properly speaking, physiological, a prospect of friendship with Germans or Russians even in the most distant future is unthinkable. Any alliance of heart and mind would be a monstrous thing, and monsters, as we all know, cannot live. You can't base your conduct on a monstrous conception. We are either worth or not worth preserving, but the horrible psychology of the situation is enough to drive the national mind to distraction. Yet under a destructive pressure, of which Western Europe can have no notion, applied by forces that were not only crushing but corrupting, we have preserved our sanity. Therefore there can be no fear of our losing our minds simply because the pressure is removed. We have neither lost our heads nor yet our moral sense. Oppression, not merely political, but affecting social relations, family life, the deepest affections of human nature, and the very fount of natural emotions, has never made us vengeful. It is worthy of notice that with every incentive present in our emotional reactions we had no recourse to political assassination. Arms in hand, hopeless or hopefully, and always against immeasurable odds, we did affirm ourselves and the justice of our cause; but wild justice has never been a part of our conception of national manliness. In all the history of Polish oppression there was only one shot fired which was not in battle. Only one! And the man who fired it in Paris at the Emperor Alexander II. was but an individual connected with no organisation, representing no shade of Polish opinion. The only effect in Poland was that of profound regret, not at the failure, but at the mere fact of the attempt. The history of our captivity is free from that stain; and whatever follies in the eyes of the world we may have perpetrated, we have neither murdered our enemies nor acted treacherously against them, nor yet have been reduced to the point of cursing each other."

I could not gainsay the truth of that discourse, I saw as clearly as my interlocutor the impossibility of the faintest sympathetic bond between Poland and her neighbours ever being formed in the future. The only course that remains to a reconstituted Poland is the elaboration, establishment, and preservation of the most correct method of political relations with neighbours to whom Poland's existence is bound to be a humiliation and an offence. Calmly considered it is an appalling task, yet one may put one's trust in that national temperament which is so completely free from aggressiveness and revenge. Therein lie the foundations of all hope. The success of renewed life for that nation whose fate is to remain in exile, ever isolated from the West, amongst hostile surroundings, depends on the sympathetic understanding of its problems by its distant friends, the Western Powers, which in their democratic development must recognise the moral and intellectual kinship of that distant outpost of their own type of civilisation, which was the only basis of Polish culture.

Whatever may be the future of Russia and the final organisation of Germany, the old hostility must remain unappeased, the fundamental antagonism must endure for years to come. The Crime of the Partition was committed by autocratic Governments which were the Governments of their time; but those Governments were characterised in the past, as they will be in the future, by their people's national traits, which remain utterly incompatible with the Polish mentality and Polish sentiment. Both the German submissiveness (idealistic as it may be) and the Russian lawlessness (fed on the corruption of all the virtues) are utterly foreign to the Polish nation, whose qualities and defects are altogether of another kind, tending to a certain exaggeration of individualism and, perhaps, to an extreme belief in the Governing Power of Free Assent: the one invariably vital principle in the internal government of the Old Republic. There was never a history more free from political bloodshed than the history of the Polish State, which never knew either feudal institutions or feudal quarrels. At the time when heads were falling on the scaffolds all over Europe there was only one political execution in Poland—only one; and as to that there still exists a tradition that the great Chancellor who democratised Polish institutions, and had to order it in pursuance of his political purpose, could not settle that matter with his conscience till the day of his death. Poland, too, had her civil wars, but this can hardly be made a matter of reproach to her by the rest of the world. Conducted with humanity, they left behind them no animosities and no sense of repression, and certainly no legacy of hatred. They were but a recognised argument in political discussion and tended always towards conciliation.

I cannot imagine, whatever form of democratic government Poland elaborates for itself, that either the nation or its leaders would do anything but welcome the closest scrutiny of their renewed political existence. The difficulty of the problem of that existence will be so great that some errors will be unavoidable, and one may be sure that they will be taken advantage of by its neighbours to discredit that living witness to a great historical crime. If not the actual frontiers, then the moral integrity of the new State is sure to be assailed before the eyes of Europe. Economical enmity will also come into play when the world's work is resumed again and competition asserts its power. Charges of aggression are certain to be made, especially as related to the small States formed of the territories of the Old Republic. And everybody knows the power of lies which go about clothed in coats of many colours, whereas, as is well known, Truth has no such advantage, and for that reason is often suppressed as not altogether proper for everyday purposes. It is not often recognised, because it is not always fit to be seen.

Already there are innuendoes, threats, hints thrown out, and even awful instances fabricated out of inadequate materials, but it is historically unthinkable that the Poland of the future, with its sacred tradition of freedom and its hereditary sense of respect for the rights of individuals and States, should seek its prosperity in aggressive action or in moral violence against that part of its once fellow-citizens who are Ruthenians or Lithuanians. The only influence that cannot be restrained is simply the influence of time, which disengages truth from all facts with a merciless logic and prevails over the passing opinions, the changing impulses of men. There can be no doubt that the moral impulses and the material interests of the new nationalities, which seem to play now the game of disintegration for the benefit of the world's enemies, will in the end bring them nearer to the Poland of this war's creation, will unite them sooner or later by a spontaneous movement towards the State which had adopted and brought them up in the development of its own humane culture—the offspring of the West.

A NOTE ON THE POLISH PROBLEM—1916

We must start from the assumption that promises made by proclamation at the beginning of this war may be binding on the individuals who made them under the stress of coming events, but cannot be regarded as binding the Governments after the end of the war.

Poland has been presented with three proclamations. Two of them were in such contrast with the avowed principles and the historic action for the last hundred years (since the Congress of Vienna) of the Powers concerned, that they were more like cynical insults to the nation's deepest feelings, its memory and its intelligence, than state papers of a conciliatory nature.

The German promises awoke nothing but indignant contempt; the Russian a bitter incredulity of the most complete kind. The Austrian proclamation, which made no promises and contented itself with pointing out the Austro- Polish relations for the last forty-five years, was received in silence. For it is a fact that in Austrian Poland alone Polish nationality was recognised as an element of the Empire, and individuals could breathe the air of freedom, of civil life, if not of political independence.

But for Poles to be Germanophile is unthinkable. To be Russophile or Austrophile is at best a counsel of despair in view of a European situation which, because of the grouping of the powers, seems to shut from them every hope, expressed or unexpressed, of a national future nursed through more than a hundred years of suffering and oppression.

Through most of these years, and especially since 1830, Poland (I use this expression since Poland exists as a spiritual entity to-day as definitely as it ever existed in her past) has put her faith in the Western Powers. Politically it may have been nothing more than a consoling illusion, and the nation had a half-consciousness of this. But what Poland was looking for from the Western Powers without discouragement and with unbroken confidence was moral support.

This is a fact of the sentimental order. But such facts have their positive value, for their idealism derives from perhaps the highest kind of reality. A sentiment asserts its claim by its force, persistence and universality. In Poland that sentimental attitude towards the Western Powers is universal. It extends to all classes. The very children are affected by it as soon as they begin to think.

The political value of such a sentiment consists in this, that it is based on profound resemblances. Therefore one can build on it as if it were a material fact. For the same reason it would be unsafe to disregard it if one proposed to build solidly. The Poles, whom superficial or ill-informed theorists are trying to force into the social and psychological formula of Slavonism, are in truth not Slavonic at all. In temperament, in feeling, in mind, and even in unreason, they are Western, with an absolute comprehension of all Western modes of thought, even of those which are remote from their historical experience.

That element of racial unity which may be called Polonism, remained compressed between Prussian Germanism on one side and the Russian

Slavonism on the other. For Germanism it feels nothing but hatred. But between Polonism and Slavonism there is not so much hatred as a complete and ineradicable incompatibility.

No political work of reconstructing Poland either as a matter of justice or expediency could be sound which would leave the new creation in dependence to Germanism or to Slavonism.

The first need not be considered. The second must be—unless the Powers elect to drop the Polish question either under the cover of vague assurances or without any disguise whatever.

But if it is considered it will be seen at once that the Slavonic solution of the Polish Question can offer no guarantees of duration or hold the promise of security for the peace of Europe.

The only basis for it would be the Grand Duke's Manifesto. But that Manifesto, signed by a personage now removed from Europe to Asia, and by a man, moreover, who if true to himself, to his conception of patriotism and to his family tradition could not have put his hand to it with any sincerity of purpose, is now divested of all authority. The forcible vagueness of its promises, its startling inconsistency with the hundred years of ruthlessly denationalising oppression permit one to doubt whether it was ever meant to have any authority.

But in any case it could have had no effect. The very nature of things would have brought to nought its professed intentions.

It is impossible to suppose that a State of Russia's power and antecedents would tolerate a privileged community (of, to Russia, unnational complexion) within the body of the Empire. All history shows that such an arrangement, however hedged in by the most solemn treaties and declarations, cannot last. In this case it would lead to a tragic issue. The absorption of Polonism is unthinkable. The last hundred years of European History proves it undeniably. There remains then extirpation, a process of blood and iron; and the last act of the Polish drama would be played then before a Europe too weary to interfere, and to the applause of Germany.

It would not be just to say that the disappearance of Polonism would add any strength to the Slavonic power of expansion. It would add no strength, but it would remove a possibly effective barrier against the surprises the future of Europe may hold in store for the Western Powers.

Thus the question whether Polonism is worth saving presents itself as a problem of politics with a practical bearing on the stability of European peace— as a barrier or perhaps better (in view of its detached position) as an outpost of the Western Powers placed between the great might of Slavonism which has not yet made up its mind to anything, and the organised Germanism which has spoken its mind with no uncertain voice, before the world.

Looked at in that light alone Polonism seems worth saving. That it has lived so long on its trust in the moral support of the Western Powers may give it another and even stronger claim, based on a truth of a more profound kind. Polonism had resisted the utmost efforts of Germanism and Slavonism for more than a hundred years. Why? Because of the strength of its ideals conscious of their kinship with the West. Such a power of resistance creates a moral obligation which it would be unsafe to neglect. There is always a risk in throwing away a tool of proved temper.

In this profound conviction of the practical and ideal worth of Polonism one approaches the problem of its preservation with a very vivid sense of the practical difficulties derived from the grouping of the Powers. The uncertainty of the extent and of the actual form of victory for the Allies will increase the difficulty of formulating a plan of Polish regeneration at the present moment.

Poland, to strike its roots again into the soil of political Europe, will require a guarantee of security for the healthy development and for the untrammelled play of such institutions as she may be enabled to give to herself.

Those institutions will be animated by the spirit of Polonism, which, having been a factor in the history of Europe and having proved its vitality under oppression, has established its right to live. That spirit, despised and hated by Germany and incompatible with Slavonism because of moral differences, cannot avoid being (in its renewed assertion) an object of dislike and mistrust.

As an unavoidable consequence of the past Poland will have to begin its existence in an atmosphere of enmities and suspicions. That advanced outpost of Western civilisation will have to hold its ground in the midst of hostile camps: always its historical fate.

Against the menace of such a specially dangerous situation the paper and ink of public Treaties cannot be an effective defence. Nothing but the actual, living, active participation of the two Western Powers in the establishment of the new Polish commonwealth, and in the first twenty years of its existence, will give the Poles a sufficient guarantee of security in the work of restoring their national life.

An Anglo-French protectorate would be the ideal form of moral and material support. But Russia, as an ally, must take her place in it on such a footing as will allay to the fullest extent her possible apprehensions and satisfy her national sentiment. That necessity will have to be formally recognised.

In reality Russia has ceased to care much for her Polish possessions. Public recognition of a mistake in political morality and a voluntary surrender of territory in the cause of European concord, cannot damage the prestige of a powerful State. The new spheres of expansion in regions more easily assimilable, will more than compensate Russia for the loss of territory on the Western frontier of the Empire.

The experience of Dual Controls and similar combinations has been so unfortunate in the past that the suggestion of a Triple Protectorate may well appear at first sight monstrous even to unprejudiced minds. But it must be remembered that this is a unique case and a problem altogether exceptional, justifying the employment of exceptional means for its solution. To those who would doubt the possibility of even bringing such a scheme into existence the answer may be made that there are psychological moments when any measure tending towards the ends of concord and justice may be brought into being.

And it seems that the end of the war would be the moment for bringing into being the political scheme advocated in this note.

Its success must depend on the singleness of purpose in the contracting Powers, and on the wisdom, the tact, the abilities, the good-will of men entrusted with its initiation and its further control. Finally it may be pointed out that this plan is the only one offering serious guarantees to all the parties occupying their respective positions within the scheme.

If her existence as a state is admitted as just, expedient and necessary, Poland has the moral right to receive her constitution not from the hand of an old enemy, but from the Western Powers alone, though of course with the fullest concurrence of Russia.

This constitution, elaborated by a committee of Poles nominated by the three Governments, will (after due discussion and amendment by the High Commissioners of the Protecting Powers) be presented to Poland as the initial document, the charter of her new life, freely offered and unreservedly accepted.

It should be as simple and short as a written constitution can be— establishing the Polish Commonwealth, settling the lines of representative institutions, the form of judicature, and leaving the greatest measure possible of self-government to the provinces forming part of the re-created Poland.

This constitution will be promulgated immediately after the three Powers had settled the frontiers of the new State, including the town of Danzic (free port) and a proportion of seaboard. The legislature will then be called together and a general treaty will regulate Poland's international portion as a protected state, the status of the High Commissioners and such-like matters. The legislature will ratify, thus making Poland, as it were, a party in the establishment of the protectorate. A point of importance.

Other general treaties will define Poland's position in the Anglo-Franco-Russian alliance, fix the numbers of the army, and settle the participation of the Powers in its organisation and training.

POLAND REVISITED—1915

I.

I have never believed in political assassination as a means to an end, and least of all in assassination of the dynastic order. I don't know how far murder can ever approach the perfection of a fine art, but looked upon with the cold eye of reason it seems but a crude expedient of impatient hope or hurried despair. There are few men whose premature death could influence human affairs more than on the surface. The deeper stream of causes depends not on individuals who, like the mass of mankind, are carried on by a destiny which no murder has ever been able to placate, divert, or arrest.

In July of last year I was a stranger in a strange city in the Midlands and particularly out of touch with the world's politics. Never a very diligent reader of newspapers, there were at that time reasons of a private order which caused me to be even less informed than usual on public affairs as presented from day to day in that necessarily atmosphereless, perspectiveless manner of the daily papers, which somehow, for a man possessed of some historic sense, robs them of all real interest. I don't think I had looked at a daily for a month past.

But though a stranger in a strange city I was not lonely, thanks to a friend who had travelled there out of pure kindness to bear me company in a conjuncture which, in a most private sense, was somewhat trying.

It was this friend who, one morning at breakfast, informed me of the murder of the Archduke Ferdinand.

The impression was mediocre. I was barely aware that such a man existed. I remembered only that not long before he had visited London. The recollection was rather of a cloud of insignificant printed words his presence in this country provoked.

Various opinions had been expressed of him, but his importance was Archducal, dynastic, purely accidental. Can there be in the world of real men anything more shadowy than an Archduke? And now he was no more; removed with an atrocity of circumstances which made one more sensible of his humanity than when he was in life. I connected that crime with Balkanic plots and aspirations so little that I had actually to ask where it had happened. My friend told me it was in Serajevo, and wondered what would be the consequences of that grave event. He asked me what I thought would happen next.

It was with perfect sincerity that I answered "Nothing," and having a great repugnance to consider murder as a factor of politics, I dismissed the subject. It fitted with my ethical sense that an act cruel and absurd should be also useless. I had also the vision of a crowd of shadowy Archdukes in the background, out of which one would step forward to take the place of that dead man in the light of the European stage. And then, to speak the whole truth, there was no man capable of forming a judgment who attended so little to the march of events as I did at that time. What for want of a more definite term I must call my mind was fixed upon my own affairs, not because they were in a bad posture, but because of their fascinating holiday-promising aspect. I had been obtaining my information as to Europe at second hand, from friends good enough to come down now and then to see us. They arrived with their pockets full of crumpled newspapers, and answered my queries casually, with gentle smiles of scepticism as to the reality of my interest. And yet I was not indifferent; but the tension in the Balkans had become chronic after the acute crisis, and one could not help being less conscious of it. It had wearied out one's attention. Who could have guessed that on that wild stage we had just been looking at a miniature rehearsal of the great world-drama, the reduced model of the very passions and violences of what the future held in store for the Powers of the Old World? Here and there, perhaps, rare minds had a suspicion of that possibility, while they watched Old Europe stage-managing fussily by means of notes and conferences, the prophetic reproduction of its awaiting fate. It was wonderfully exact in the spirit; same roar of guns, same protestations of superiority, same words in the air; race, liberation, justice—and the same mood of trivial demonstrations. One could not take to-day a ticket for Petersburg. "You mean Petrograd," would say the booking clerk. Shortly after the fall of Adrianople a friend of mine passing through Sophia asked for some *cafe turc* at the end of his lunch.

"Monsieur veut dire Cafe balkanique," the patriotic waiter corrected him austerely.

I will not say that I had not observed something of that instructive aspect of the war of the Balkans both in its first and in its second phase. But those with whom I touched upon that vision were pleased to see in it the evidence of my alarmist cynicism. As to alarm, I pointed out that fear is natural to man, and even salutary. It has done as much as courage for the preservation of races and institutions. But from a charge of cynicism I have always shrunk instinctively. It is like a charge of being blind in one eye, a moral disablement, a sort of disgraceful calamity that must he carried off with a jaunty bearing—a sort of thing I am not capable of. Rather than be thought a mere jaunty cripple I allowed myself to be blinded by the gross obviousness of the usual arguments. It was pointed out to me that these Eastern nations were not far removed from a savage state. Their economics were yet at the stage of scratching the earth and feeding the pigs. The highly-developed material civilisation of Europe could not allow itself to be disturbed by a war. The industry and the finance could not allow themselves to be disorganised by the ambitions of an idle class, or even the aspirations, whatever they might be, of the masses.

Very plausible all this sounded. War does not pay. There had been a book written on that theme—an attempt to put pacificism on a material basis. Nothing more solid in the way of argument could have been advanced on this trading and manufacturing globe. War was "bad business!" This was final.

But, truth to say, on this July day I reflected but little on the condition of the civilised world. Whatever sinister passions were heaving under its splendid and complex surface, I was too agitated by a simple and innocent desire of my own, to notice the signs or interpret them correctly. The most innocent of passions will take the edge off one's judgment. The desire which possessed me was simply the desire to travel. And that being so it would have taken something very plain in the way of symptoms to shake my simple trust in the stability of things on the Continent. My sentiment and not my reason was engaged there. My eyes were turned to the past, not to the future; the past that one cannot suspect and mistrust, the shadowy and unquestionable moral possession the darkest struggles of which wear a halo of glory and peace.

In the preceding month of May we had received an invitation to spend some weeks in Poland in a country house in the neighbourhood of Cracow, but within the Russian frontier. The enterprise at first seemed to me considerable. Since leaving the sea, to which I have been faithful for so many years, I have discovered that there is in my composition very little stuff from which travellers are made. I confess that my first impulse about a projected journey is to leave it alone. But the invitation received at first with a sort of dismay ended by rousing the dormant energy of my feelings. Cracow is the town where I spent with my father the last eighteen months of his life. It was in that old royal and academical city that I ceased to be a child, became a boy, had known the friendships, the admirations, the thoughts and the indignations of that age. It was within those historical walls that I began to understand things, form affections, lay up a store of memories and a fund of sensations with which I was to break violently by throwing myself into an unrelated existence. It was like the experience of another world. The wings of time made a great dusk over all this, and I feared at first that if I ventured bodily in there I would discover that I who have had to do with a good many imaginary lives have been embracing mere shadows in my youth. I feared. But fear in itself may become a fascination. Men have gone, alone and trembling, into graveyards at midnight—just to see what would happen. And this adventure was to be pursued in sunshine. Neither would it be pursued alone. The invitation was extended to us all. This journey would have something of a migratory character, the invasion of a tribe. My present, all that gave solidity and value to it, at any rate, would stand by me in this test of the reality of my past. I was pleased with the idea of showing my companions what Polish country life was like; to visit the town where I was at school before the boys by my side should grow too old, and gaining an individual past of their own, should lose their unsophisticated interest in mine. It is only in the short instants of early youth that we have the faculty of coming out of ourselves to see dimly the visions and share the emotions of another soul. For youth all is reality in this world, and with justice, since it apprehends so vividly its images behind which a longer life makes one doubt whether there is any substance. I trusted to the fresh receptivity of these young beings in whom, unless Heredity is an empty word, there should have been a fibre which would answer to the sight, to the atmosphere, to the memories of that corner of the earth where my own boyhood had received its earliest independent impressions.

The first days of the third week in July, while the telegraph wires hummed with the words of enormous import which were to fill blue books, yellow books, white books, and to arouse the wonder of mankind, passed for us in light-hearted preparations for the journey. What was it but just a rush through Germany, to get across as quickly as possible?

Germany is the part of the earth's solid surface of which I know the least. In all my life I had been across it only twice. I may well say of it *vidi tantum*; and the very little I saw was through the window of a railway carriage at express speed. Those journeys of mine had been more like pilgrimages when one hurries on towards the goal for the satisfaction of a deeper need than curiosity. In this last instance, too, I was so incurious that I would have liked to have fallen asleep on the shores of England and opened my eyes, if it were possible, only on the other side of the Silesian frontier. Yet, in truth, as many others have done, I had "sensed it"—that promised land of steel, of chemical dyes, of method, of efficiency; that race planted in the middle of Europe, assuming in grotesque vanity the attitude of Europeans amongst effete Asiatics or barbarous niggers; and, with a consciousness of superiority freeing their hands from all moral bonds, anxious to take up, if I may express myself so, the "perfect man's burden." Meantime, in a clearing of the Teutonic forest, their sages were rearing a Tree of Cynical Wisdom, a sort of Upas tree, whose shade may be seen now lying over the prostrate body of Belgium. It must be said that they laboured openly enough, watering it with the most authentic sources of all madness, and watching with their be-spectacled eyes the slow ripening of the glorious blood-red fruit. The sincerest words of peace, words of menace, and I verily believe words of abasement, even if there had been a voice vile enough to utter them, would have been wasted on their ecstasy. For when the fruit ripens on a branch it must fall. There is nothing on earth that can prevent it.

II.

For reasons which at first seemed to me somewhat obscure, that one of my companions whose wishes are law decided that our travels should begin in an unusual way by the crossing of the North Sea. We should proceed from Harwich to Hamburg. Besides being thirty-six times longer than the Dover-Calais passage this rather unusual route had an air of adventure in better keeping with the romantic feeling of this Polish journey which for so many years had been before us in a state of a project full of colour and promise, but always retreating, elusive like an enticing mirage.

And, after all, it had turned out to be no mirage. No wonder they were excited. It's no mean experience to lay your hands on a mirage. The day of departure had come, the very hour had struck. The luggage was coming downstairs. It was most convincing. Poland then, if erased from the map, yet existed in reality; it was not a mere *pays du reve*, where you can travel only in imagination. For no man, they argued, not even father, an habitual pursuer of dreams, would push the love of the novelist's art of make-believe to the point of burdening himself with real trunks for a voyage *au pays du reve*.

As we left the door of our house, nestling in, perhaps, the most peaceful nook in Kent, the sky, after weeks of perfectly brazen serenity, veiled its blue depths and started to weep fine tears for the refreshment of the parched fields. A pearly blur settled over them, and a light sifted of all glare, of everything unkindly and searching that dwells in the splendour of unveiled skies. All unconscious of going towards the very scenes of war, I carried off in my eye, this tiny fragment of Great Britain; a few fields, a wooded rise; a clump of trees or two, with a short stretch of road, and here and there a gleam of red wall and tiled roof above the darkening hedges wrapped up in soft mist and peace. And I felt that all this had a very strong hold on me as the embodiment of a beneficent and gentle spirit; that it was dear to me not as an inheritance, but as an acquisition, as a conquest in the sense in which a woman is conquered—by love, which is a sort of surrender.

These were strange, as if disproportionate thoughts to the matter in hand, which was the simplest sort of a Continental holiday. And I am certain that my companions, near as they are to me, felt no other trouble but the suppressed excitement of pleasurable anticipation. The forms and the spirit of the land before their eyes were their inheritance, not their conquest—which is a thing precarious, and, therefore, the most precious, possessing you if only by the fear of unworthiness rather than possessed by you. Moreover, as we sat together in the same railway carriage, they were looking forward to a voyage in space, whereas I felt more and more plainly, that what I had started on was a journey in time, into the past; a fearful enough prospect for the most consistent, but to him who had not known how to preserve against his impulses the order and continuity of his life—so that at times it presented itself to his conscience as a series of betrayals—still more dreadful.

I down here these thoughts so exclusively personal, to explain why there was no room in my consciousness for the apprehension of a European war. I don't mean to say that I ignored the possibility; I simply did not think of it. And it made no difference; for if I had thought of it, it could only have been in the lame and inconclusive way of the common uninitiated mortals; and I am sure that nothing short of intellectual certitude—obviously unattainable by the man in the street—could have stayed me on that journey which now that I had started on it seemed an irrevocable thing, a necessity of my self-respect.

London, the London before the war, flaunting its enormous glare, as of a monstrous conflagration up into the black sky—with its best Venice-like aspect of rainy evenings, the wet asphalted streets lying with the sheen of sleeping water in winding canals, and the great houses of the city towering all dark, like empty palaces, above the reflected lights of the glistening roadway.

Everything in the subdued incomplete night-life around the Mansion House went on normally with its fascinating air of a dead commercial city of sombre walls through which the inextinguishable activity of its millions streamed East and West in a brilliant flow of lighted vehicles.

In Liverpool Street, as usual too, through the double gates, a continuous line of taxi-cabs glided down the inclined approach and up again, like an endless chain of dredger-buckets, pouring in the passengers, and dipping them out of the great railway station under the inexorable pallid face of the clock telling off the diminishing minutes of peace. It was the hour of the boat-trains to Holland, to Hamburg, and there seemed to be no lack of people, fearless, reckless, or ignorant, who wanted to go to these places. The station was normally crowded, and if there was a great flutter of evening papers in the multitude of hands there were no signs of extraordinary emotion on that multitude of faces. There was nothing in them to distract me from the thought that it was singularly appropriate that I should start from this station on the retraced way of my existence. For this was the station at which, thirty-seven years before, I arrived on my first visit to London. Not the same building, but the same spot. At nineteen years of age, after a period of probation and training I had imposed upon myself as ordinary seaman on board a North Sea coaster, I had come up from Lowestoft—my first long railway journey in England—to "sign on" for an Antipodean voyage in a deep-water ship. Straight from a railway carriage I had walked into the great city with something of the feeling of a traveller penetrating into a vast and unexplored wilderness. No explorer could have been more lonely. I did not know a single soul of all these millions that all around me peopled the mysterious distances of the streets. I cannot say I was free from a little youthful awe, but at that age one's feelings are simple. I was elated. I was pursuing a clear aim, I was carrying out a deliberate plan of making out of myself, in the first place, a seaman worthy of the service, good enough to work by the side of the men with whom I was to live; and in the second place, I had to justify my existence to myself, to redeem a tacit moral pledge. Both these aims were to be attained by the same effort. How simple seemed the problem of life then, on that hazy day of early September in the year 1878, when I entered London for the first time.

From that point of view—Youth and a straightforward scheme of conduct—it was certainly a year of grace. All the help I had to get in touch with the world I was invading was a piece of paper not much bigger than the palm of my hand—in which I held it—torn out of a larger plan of London for the greater facility of reference. It had been the object of careful study for some days past. The fact that I could take a conveyance at the station never occurred to my mind, no, not even when I got out into the street, and stood, taking my anxious bearings, in the midst, so to speak, of twenty thousand hansoms. A strange absence of mind or unconscious conviction that one cannot approach an important moment of one's life by means of a hired carriage? Yes, it would have been a preposterous proceeding. And indeed I was to make an Australian voyage and encircle the globe before ever entering a London hansom.

Another document, a cutting from a newspaper, containing the address of an obscure shipping agent, was in my pocket. And I needed not to take it out. That address was as if graven deep in my brain. I muttered its words to myself as I walked on, navigating the sea of London by the chart concealed in the palm of my hand; for I had vowed to myself not to inquire my way from anyone. Youth is the time of rash pledges. Had I taken a wrong turning I would have been lost; and if faithful to my pledge I might have remained lost for days, for weeks, have left perhaps my bones to be discovered bleaching in some blind alley of the Whitechapel district, as it had happened to lonely travellers lost in the bush. But I walked on to my destination without hesitation or mistake, showing there, for the first time, some of that faculty to absorb and make my own the imaged topography of a chart, which in later years was to help me in regions of intricate navigation to keep the ships entrusted to me off the ground. The place I was bound to was not easy to find. It was one of those courts hidden away from the charted and navigable streets, lost among the thick growth of houses like a dark pool in the depths of a forest, approached by an inconspicuous archway as if by secret path; a Dickensian nook of London, that wonder city, the growth of which bears no sign of intelligent design, but many traces of freakishly sombre phantasy the Great Master knew so well how to bring out by the magic of his understanding love. And the office I entered was Dickensian too. The dust of the Waterloo year lay on the panes and frames of its windows; early Georgian grime clung to its sombre wainscoting.

It was one o'clock in the afternoon, but the day was gloomy. By the light of a single gas-jet depending from the smoked ceiling I saw an elderly man, in a long coat of black broadcloth. He had a grey beard, a big nose, thick lips, and heavy shoulders. His curly white hair and the general character of his head recalled vaguely a burly apostle in the *barocco* style of Italian art. Standing up at a tall, shabby, slanting desk, his silver-rimmed spectacles pushed up high on his forehead, he was eating a mutton-chop, which had been just brought to him from some Dickensian eating-house round the corner.

Without ceasing to eat he turned to me his florid, *barocco* apostle's face with an expression of inquiry.

I produced elaborately a series of vocal sounds which must have borne sufficient resemblance to the phonetics of English speech, for his face broke into a smile of comprehension almost at once.—"Oh, it's you who wrote a letter to me the other day from Lowestoft about getting a ship."

I had written to him from Lowestoft. I can't remember a single word of that letter now. It was my very first composition in the English language. And he had understood it, evidently, for he spoke to the point at once, explaining that his business, mainly, was to find good ships for young gentlemen who wanted to go to sea as premium apprentices with a view of being trained for officers. But he gathered that this was not my object. I did not desire to be apprenticed. Was that the case?

It was. He was good enough to say then, "Of course I see that you are a gentleman. But your wish is to get a berth before the mast as an Able Seaman if possible. Is that it?"

It was certainly my wish; but he stated doubtfully that he feared he could not help me much in this. There was an Act of Parliament which made it penal to procure ships for sailors. "An Act-of-Parliament. A law," he took pains to impress it again and again on my foreign understanding, while I looked at him in consternation.

I had not been half an hour in London before I had run my head against an Act of Parliament! What a hopeless adventure! However, the *barocco* apostle was a resourceful person in his way, and we managed to get round the hard letter of it without damage to its fine spirit. Yet, strictly speaking, it was not the conduct of a good citizen; and in retrospect there is an unfilial flavour about that early sin of mine. For this Act of Parliament, the Merchant Shipping Act of the Victorian era, had been in a manner of speaking a father and mother to me. For many years it had regulated and disciplined my life, prescribed my food and the amount of my breathing space, had looked after my health and tried as much as possible to secure my personal safety in a risky calling. It isn't such a bad thing to lead a life of hard toil and plain duty within the four corners of an honest Act of Parliament. And I am glad to say that its seventies have never been applied to me.

In the year 1878, the year of "Peace with Honour," I had walked as lone as any human being in the streets of London, out of Liverpool Street Station, to surrender myself to its care. And now, in the year of the war waged for honour and conscience more than for any other cause, I was there again, no longer alone, but a man of infinitely dear and close ties grown since that time, of work done, of words written, of friendships secured. It was like the closing of a thirty-six-year cycle.

All unaware of the War Angel already awaiting, with the trumpet at his lips, the stroke of the fatal hour, I sat there, thinking that this life of ours is neither long nor short, but that it can appear very wonderful, entertaining, and pathetic, with symbolic images and bizarre associations crowded into one half-hour of retrospective musing.

I felt, too, that this journey, so suddenly entered upon, was bound to take me away from daily life's actualities at every step. I felt it more than ever when presently we steamed out into the North Sea, on a dark night fitful with gusts of wind, and I lingered on deck, alone of all the tale of the ship's passengers. That sea was to me something unforgettable, something much more than a name. It had been for some time the schoolroom of my trade. On it, I may safely say, I had learned, too, my first words of English. A wild and stormy abode, sometimes, was that confined, shallow-water academy of seamanship from which I launched myself on the wide oceans. My teachers had been the sailors of the Norfolk shore; coast men, with steady eyes, mighty limbs, and gentle voice; men of very few words, which at least were never bare of meaning. Honest, strong, steady men, sobered by domestic ties, one and all, as far as I can remember.

That is what years ago the North Sea I could hear growling in the dark all round the ship had been for me. And I fancied that I must have been carrying its voice in my ear ever since, for nothing could be more familiar than those short, angry sounds I was listening to with a smile of affectionate recognition.

I could not guess that before many days my old schoolroom would be desecrated by violence, littered with wrecks, with death walking its waves, hiding under its waters. Perhaps while I am writing these words the children, or maybe the grandchildren, of my pacific teachers are out in trawlers, under the Naval flag, dredging for German submarine mines.

III.

I have said that the North Sea was my finishing school of seamanship before I launched myself on the wider oceans. Confined as it is in comparison with the vast stage of this water-girt globe, I did not know it in all its parts. My classroom was the region of the English East Coast which, in the year of Peace with Honour, had long forgotten the war episodes belonging to its maritime history. It was a peaceful coast, agricultural, industrial, the home of fishermen. At night the lights of its many towns played on the clouds, or in clear weather lay still, here and there, in brilliant pools above the ink-black outline of the land. On many a night I have hauled at the braces under the shadow of that coast, envying, as sailors will, the people on shore sleeping quietly in their beds within sound of the sea. I imagine that not one head on those envied pillows was made uneasy by the slightest premonition of the realities of naval war the short lifetime of one generation was to bring so close to their homes.

Though far away from that region of kindly memories and traversing a part of the North Sea much less known to me, I was deeply conscious of the familiarity of my surroundings. It was a cloudy, nasty day: and the aspects of Nature don't change, unless in the course of thousands of years—or, perhaps, centuries. The Phoenicians, its first discoverers, the Romans, the first imperial rulers of that sea, had experienced days like this, so different in the wintry quality of the light, even on a July afternoon, from anything they had ever known in their native Mediterranean. For myself, a very late comer into that sea, and its former pupil, I accorded amused recognition to the characteristic aspect so well remembered from my days of training. The same old thing. A grey- green expanse of smudgy waters grinning angrily at one with white foam- ridges, and over all a cheerless, unglowing canopy, apparently made of wet blotting-paper. From time to time a flurry of fine rain blew along like a puff of smoke across the dots of distant fishing boats, very few, very scattered, and tossing restlessly on an ever dissolving, ever re- forming sky-line.

Those flurries, and the steady rolling of the ship, accounted for the emptiness of the decks, favouring my reminiscent mood. It might have been a day of five and thirty years ago, when there were on this and every other sea more sails and less smoke-stacks to be seen. Yet, thanks to the unchangeable sea I could have given myself up to the illusion of a revised past, had it not been for the periodical transit across my gaze of a German passenger. He was marching round and round the boat deck with characteristic determination. Two sturdy boys gambolled round him in his progress like two disorderly satellites round their parent planet. He was bringing them home, from their school in England, for their holiday. What could have induced such a sound Teuton to entrust his offspring to the unhealthy influences of that effete, corrupt, rotten and criminal country I cannot imagine. It could hardly have been from motives of economy. I did not speak to him. He trod the deck of that decadent British ship with a scornful foot while his breast (and to a large extent his stomach, too) appeared expanded by the consciousness of a superior destiny. Later I could observe the same truculent bearing, touched with the racial grotesqueness, in the men of the *Landwehr* corps, that passed through Cracow to reinforce the Austrian army in Eastern Galicia. Indeed, the haughty passenger might very well have been, most probably was, an officer of the *Landwehr*; and perhaps those two fine active boys are orphans by now. Thus things acquire significance by the lapse of time. A citizen, a father, a warrior, a mote in the dust-cloud of six million fighting particles, an unconsidered trifle for the jaws of war, his humanity was not consciously impressed on my mind at the time. Mainly, for me, he was a sharp tapping of heels round the corner of the deck-house, a white yachting cap and a green overcoat getting periodically between my eyes and the shifting cloud-horizon of the ashy-grey North Sea. He was but a shadowy intrusion and a disregarded one, for, far away there to the West, in the direction of the Dogger Bank, where fishermen go seeking their daily bread and sometimes find their graves, I could behold an experience of my own in the winter of '81, not of war, truly, but of a fairly lively contest with the elements which were very angry indeed.

There had been a troublesome week of it, including one hateful night—or a night of hate (it isn't for nothing that the North Sea is also called the German Ocean)—when all the fury stored in its heart seemed concentrated on one ship which could do no better than float on her side in an unnatural, disagreeable, precarious, and altogether intolerable manner. There were on board, besides myself, seventeen men all good and true, including a round enormous Dutchman who, in those hours between sunset and sunrise, managed to lose his blown-out appearance somehow, became as it were deflated, and thereafter for a good long time moved in our midst wrinkled and slack all over like a half-collapsed balloon. The whimpering of our deck-boy, a skinny, impressionable little scarecrow out of a training-ship, for whom, because of the tender immaturity of his nerves, this display of German Ocean frightfulness was too much (before the year was out he developed into a sufficiently cheeky young ruffian), his desolate whimpering, I say, heard between the gusts of that black, savage night, was much more present to my mind and indeed to my senses than the green overcoat and the white cap of the German passenger circling the deck indefatigably, attended by his two gyrating children.

"That's a very nice gentleman." This information, together with the fact that he was a widower and a regular passenger twice a year by the ship, was communicated to me suddenly by our captain. At intervals through the day he would pop out of the chart-room and offer me short snatches of conversation. He owned a simple soul and a not very entertaining mind, and he was without malice and, I believe, quite unconsciously, a warm Germanophil. And no wonder! As he told me himself, he had been fifteen years on that run, and spent almost as much of his life in Hamburg as in Harwich.

"Wonderful people they are," he repeated from time to time, without entering into particulars, but with many nods of sagacious obstinacy. What he knew of them, I suppose, were a few commercial travellers and small merchants, most likely. But I had observed long before that German genius has a hypnotising power over half-baked souls and half-lighted minds. There is an immense force of suggestion in highly organised mediocrity. Had it not hypnotised half Europe? My man was very much under the spell of German excellence. On the other hand, his contempt for France was equally general and unbounded. I tried to advance some arguments against this position, but I only succeeded in making him hostile. "I believe you are a Frenchman yourself," he snarled at last, giving me an intensely suspicious look; and forthwith broke off communications with a man of such unsound sympathies.

Hour by hour the blotting-paper sky and the great flat greenish smudge of the sea had been taking on a darker tone, without any change in their colouring and texture. Evening was coming on over the North Sea. Black uninteresting hummocks of land appeared, dotting the duskiness of water and clouds in the Eastern board: tops of islands fringing the German shore. While I was looking at their antics amongst the waves—and for all their solidity they were very elusive things in the failing light—another passenger came out on deck. This one wore a dark overcoat and a grey cap. The yellow leather strap of his binocular case crossed his chest. His elderly red cheeks nourished but a very thin crop of short white hairs, and the end of his nose was so perfectly round that it determined the whole character of his physiognomy. Indeed nothing else in it had the slightest chance to assert itself. His disposition, unlike the widower's, appeared to be mild and humane. He offered me the loan of his glasses. He had a wife and some small children concealed in the depths of the ship, and he thought they were very well where they were. His eldest son was about the decks somewhere.

"We are Americans," he remarked weightily, but in a rather peculiar tone. He spoke English with the accent of our captain's "wonderful people," and proceeded to give me the history of the family's crossing the Atlantic in a White Star liner. They remained in England just the time necessary for a railway journey from Liverpool to Harwich. His people (those in the depths of the ship) were naturally a little tired.

At that moment a young man of about twenty, his son, rushed up to us from the fore-deck in a state of intense elation. "Hurrah," he cried under his breath. "The first German light! Hurrah!"

And those two American citizens shook hands on it with the greatest fervour, while I turned away and received full in the eyes the brilliant wink of the Borkum lighthouse squatting low down in the darkness. The shade of the night had settled on the North Sea.

I do not think I have ever seen before a night so full of lights. The great change of sea life since my time was brought home to me. I had been conscious all day of an interminable procession of steamers. They went on and on as if in chase of each other, the Baltic trade, the trade of Scandinavia, of Denmark, of Germany, pitching heavily into a head sea and bound for the gateway of Dover Straits. Singly, and in small companies of two and three, they emerged from the dull, colourless, sunless distances ahead as if the supply of rather roughly finished mechanical toys were inexhaustible in some mysterious cheap store away there, below the grey curve of the earth. Cargo steam vessels have reached by this time a height of utilitarian ugliness which, when one reflects that it is the product of human ingenuity, strikes hopeless awe into one. These dismal creations look still uglier at sea than in port, and with an added touch of the ridiculous. Their rolling waddle when seen at a certain angle, their abrupt clockwork nodding in a sea-way, so unlike the soaring lift and swing of a craft under sail, have in them something caricatural, a suggestion of a low parody directed at noble predecessors by an improved generation of dull, mechanical toilers, conceited and without grace.

When they switched on (each of these unlovely cargo tanks carried tame lightning within its slab-sided body), when they switched on their lamps they spangled the night with the cheap, electric, shop-glitter, here, there, and everywhere, as of some High Street, broken up and washed out to sea. Later, Heligoland cut into the overhead darkness with its powerful beam, infinitely prolonged out of unfathomable night under the clouds.

I remained on deck until we stopped and a steam pilot-boat, so overlighted amidships that one could not make out her complete shape, glided across our bows and sent a pilot on board. I fear that the oar, as a working implement, will become presently as obsolete as the sail. The pilot boarded us in a motor-dinghy. More and more is mankind reducing its physical activities to pulling levers and twirling little wheels. Progress! Yet the older methods of meeting natural forces demanded intelligence too; an equally fine readiness of wits. And readiness of wits working in combination with the strength of muscles made a more complete man.

It was really a surprisingly small dinghy and it ran to and fro like a water-insect fussing noisily down there with immense self-importance. Within hail of us the hull of the Elbe lightship floated all dark and silent under its enormous round, service lantern; a faithful black shadow watching the broad estuary full of lights.

Such was my first view of the Elbe approached under the wings of peace ready for flight away from the luckless shores of Europe. Our visual impressions remain with us so persistently that I find it extremely difficult to hold fast to the rational belief that now everything is dark over there, that the Elbe lightship has been towed away from its post of duty, the triumphant beam of Heligoland extinguished, and the pilot-boat laid up, or turned to warlike uses for lack of its proper work to do. And obviously it must be so.

Any trickle of oversea trade that passes yet that way must be creeping along cautiously with the unlighted, war-blighted black coast close on one hand, and sudden death on the other. For all the space we steamed through that Sunday evening must now be one great minefield, sown thickly with the seeds of hate; while submarines steal out to sea, over the very spot perhaps where the insect-dinghy put a pilot on board of us with so much fussy importance. Mines; Submarines. The last word in sea-warfare! Progress—impressively disclosed by this war.

There have been other wars! Wars not inferior in the greatness of the stake and in the fierce animosity of feelings. During that one which was finished a hundred years ago it happened that while the English Fleet was keeping watch on Brest, an American, perhaps Fulton himself, offered to the Maritime Prefect of the port and to the French Admiral, an invention which would sink all the unsuspecting English ships one after another—or, at any rate most of them. The offer was not even taken into consideration; and the Prefect ends his report to the Minister in Paris with a fine phrase of indignation: "It is not the sort of death one would deal to brave men."

And behold, before history had time to hatch another war of the like proportions in the intensity of aroused passions and the greatness of issues, the dead flavour of archaism descended on the manly sentiment of those self-denying words. Mankind has been demoralised since by its own mastery of mechanical appliances. Its spirit is apparently so weak now, and its flesh has grown so strong, that it will face any deadly horror of destruction and cannot resist the temptation to use any stealthy, murderous contrivance. It has become the intoxicated slave of its own detestable ingenuity. It is true, too, that since the Napoleonic time another sort of war-doctrine has been inculcated in a nation, and held out to the world.

IV.

On this journey of ours, which for me was essentially not a progress, but a retracing of footsteps on the road of life, I had no beacons to look for in Germany. I had never lingered in that land which, on the whole, is so singularly barren of memorable manifestations of generous sympathies and magnanimous impulses. An ineradicable, invincible, provincialism of envy and vanity clings to the forms of its thought like a frowsy garment. Even while yet very young I turned my eyes away from it instinctively as from a threatening phantom. I believe that children and dogs have, in their innocence, a special power of perception as far as spectral apparitions and coming misfortunes are concerned.

I let myself be carried through Germany as if it were pure space, without sights, without sounds. No whispers of the war reached my voluntary abstraction. And perhaps not so very voluntary after all! Each of us is a fascinating spectacle to himself, and I had to watch my own personality returning from another world, as it were, to revisit the glimpses of old moons. Considering the condition of humanity, I am, perhaps, not so much to blame for giving myself up to that occupation. We prize the sensation of our continuity, and we can only capture it in that way. By watching.

We arrived in Cracow late at night. After a scrambly supper, I said to my eldest boy, "I can't go to bed. I am going out for a look round. Coming?"

He was ready enough. For him, all this was part of the interesting adventure of the whole journey. We stepped out of the portal of the hotel into an empty street, very silent and bright with moonlight. I was, indeed, revisiting the glimpses of the moon. I felt so much like a ghost that the discovery that I could remember such material things as the right turn to take and the general direction of the street gave me a moment of wistful surprise.

The street, straight and narrow, ran into the great Market Square of the town, the centre of its affairs and of the lighter side of its life. We could see at the far end of the street a promising widening of space. At the corner an unassuming (but armed) policeman, wearing ceremoniously at midnight a pair of white gloves which made his big hands extremely noticeable, turned his head to look at the grizzled foreigner holding forth in a strange tongue to a youth on whose arm he leaned.

The Square, immense in its solitude, was full to the brim of moonlight. The garland of lights at the foot of the houses seemed to burn at the bottom of a bluish pool. I noticed with infinite satisfaction that the unnecessary trees the Municipality insisted upon sticking between the stones had been steadily refusing to grow. They were not a bit bigger than the poor victims I could remember. Also, the paving operations seemed to be exactly at the same point at which I left them forty years before. There were the dull, torn-up patches on that bright expanse, the piles of paving material looking ominously black, like heads of rocks on a silvery sea. Who was it that said that Time works wonders? What an exploded superstition! As far as these trees and these paving stones were concerned, it had worked nothing. The suspicion of the unchangeableness of things already vaguely suggested to my senses by our rapid drive from the railway station was agreeably strengthened within me.

"We are now on the line A.B.," I said to my companion, importantly.

It was the name bestowed in my time on one of the sides of the Square by the senior students of that town of classical learning and historical relics. The common citizens knew nothing of it, and, even if they had, would not have dreamed of taking it seriously. He who used it was of the initiated, belonged to the Schools. We youngsters regarded that name as a fine jest, the invention of a most excellent fancy. Even as I uttered it to my boy I experienced again that sense of my privileged initiation. And then, happening to look up at the wall, I saw in the light of the corner lamp, a white, cast-iron tablet fixed thereon, bearing an inscription in raised black letters, thus: "Line A.B." Heavens! The name had been adopted officially! Any town urchin, any guttersnipe, any herb-selling woman of the market-place, any wandering Boeotian, was free to talk of the line A.B., to walk on the line A.B., to appoint to meet his friends on the line A.B. It had become a mere name in a directory. I was stunned by the extreme mutability of things. Time could work wonders, and no mistake. A Municipality had stolen an invention of excellent fancy, and a fine jest had turned into a horrid piece of cast- iron.

I proposed that we should walk to the other end of the line, using the profaned name, not only without gusto, but with positive distaste. And this, too, was one of the wonders of Time, for a bare minute had worked that change. There was at the end of the line a certain street I wanted to look at, I explained to my companion.

To our right the unequal massive towers of St. Mary's Church soared aloft into the ethereal radiance of the air, very black on their shaded sides, glowing with a soft phosphorescent sheen on the others. In the distance the Florian Gate, thick and squat under its pointed roof, barred the street with the square shoulders of the old city wall. In the narrow, brilliantly pale vista of bluish flagstones and silvery fronts of houses, its black archway stood out small and very distinct.

There was not a soul in sight, and not even the echo of a footstep for our ears. Into this coldly illuminated and dumb emptiness there issued out of my aroused memory, a small boy of eleven, wending his way, not very fast, to a preparatory school for day-pupils on the second floor of the third house down from the Florian Gate. It was in the winter months of 1868. At eight o'clock of every morning that God made, sleet or shine, I walked up Florian Street. But of that, my first school, I remember very little. I believe that one of my co-sufferers there has become a much appreciated editor of historical documents. But I didn't suffer much from the various imperfections of my first school. I was rather indifferent to school troubles. I had a private gnawing worm of my own. This was the time of my father's last illness. Every evening at seven, turning my back on the Florian Gate, I walked all the way to a big old house in a quiet narrow street a good distance beyond the Great Square. There, in a large drawing-room, panelled and bare, with heavy cornices and a lofty ceiling, in a little oasis of light made by two candles in a desert of dusk, I sat at a little table to worry and ink myself all over till the task of my preparation was done. The table of my toil faced a tall white door, which was kept closed; now and then it would come ajar and a nun in a white coif would squeeze herself through the crack, glide across the room, and disappear. There were two of these noiseless nursing nuns. Their voices were seldom heard. For, indeed, what could they have had to say? When they did speak to me it was with their lips hardly moving, in a claustral, clear whisper. Our domestic matters were ordered by the elderly housekeeper of our neighbour on the second floor, a Canon of the Cathedral, lent for the emergency. She, too, spoke but seldom. She wore a black dress with a cross hanging by a chain on her ample bosom. And though when she spoke she moved her lips more than the nuns, she never let her voice rise above a peacefully murmuring note. The air around me was all piety, resignation, and silence.

I don't know what would have become of me if I had not been a reading boy. My prep. finished I would have had nothing to do but sit and watch the awful stillness of the sick room flow out through the closed door and coldly enfold my scared heart. I suppose that in a futile childish way I would have gone crazy. But I was a reading boy. There were many books about, lying on consoles, on tables, and even on the floor, for we had not had time to settle down. I read! What did I not read! Sometimes the elder nun, gliding up and casting a mistrustful look on the open pages, would lay her hand lightly on my head and suggest in a doubtful whisper, "Perhaps it is not very good for you to read these books." I would raise my eyes to her face mutely, and with a vague gesture of giving it up she would glide away.

Later in the evening, but not always, I would be permitted to tip-toe into the sick room to say good-night to the figure prone on the bed, which often could not acknowledge my presence but by a slow movement of the eyes, put my lips dutifully to the nerveless hand lying on the coverlet, and tip-toe out again. Then I would go to bed, in a room at the end of the corridor, and often, not always, cry myself into a good sound sleep.

I looked forward to what was coming with an incredulous terror. I turned my eyes from it sometimes with success, and yet all the time I had an awful sensation of the inevitable. I had also moments of revolt which stripped off me some of my simple trust in the government of the universe. But when the inevitable entered the sick room and the white door was thrown wide open, I don't think I found a single tear to shed. I have a suspicion that the Canon's housekeeper looked on me as the most callous little wretch on earth.

The day of the funeral came in due course and all the generous "Youth of the Schools," the grave Senate of the University, the delegations of the Trade-guilds, might have obtained (if they cared) *de visu* evidence of the callousness of the little wretch. There was nothing in my aching head but a few words, some such stupid sentences as, "It's done," or, "It's accomplished" (in Polish it is much shorter), or something of the sort, repeating itself endlessly. The long procession moved out of the narrow street, down a long street, past the Gothic front of St. Mary's under its unequal towers, towards the Florian Gate.

In the moonlight-flooded silence of the old town of glorious tombs and tragic memories, I could see again the small boy of that day following a hearse; a space kept clear in which I walked alone, conscious of an enormous following, the clumsy swaying of the tall black machine, the chanting of the surpliced clergy at the head, the flames of tapers passing under the low archway of the gate, the rows of bared heads on the pavements with fixed, serious eyes. Half the population had turned out on that fine May afternoon. They had not come to honour a great achievement, or even some splendid failure. The dead and they were victims alike of an unrelenting destiny which cut them off from every path of merit and glory. They had come only to render homage to the ardent fidelity of the man whose life had been a fearless confession in word and deed of a creed which the simplest heart in that crowd could feel and understand.

It seemed to me that if I remained longer there in that narrow street I should become the helpless prey of the Shadows I had called up. They were crowding upon me, enigmatic and insistent in their clinging air of the grave that tasted of dust and of the bitter vanity of old hopes.

"Let's go back to the hotel, my boy," I said. "It's getting late."

It will be easily understood that I neither thought nor dreamt that night of a possible war. For the next two days I went about amongst my fellow men, who welcomed me with the utmost consideration and friendliness, but unanimously derided my fears of a war. They would not believe in it. It was impossible. On the evening of the second day I was in the hotel's smoking room, an irrationally private apartment, a sanctuary for a few choice minds of the town, always pervaded by a dim religious light, and more hushed than any club reading-room I have ever been in. Gathered into a small knot, we were discussing the situation in subdued tones suitable to the genius of the place.

A gentleman with a fine head of white hair suddenly pointed an impatient finger in my direction and apostrophised me.

"What I want to know is whether, should there be war, England would come in."

The time to draw a breath, and I spoke out for the Cabinet without faltering.

"Most assuredly. I should think all Europe knows that by this time."

He took hold of the lapel of my coat, and, giving it a slight jerk for greater emphasis, said forcibly:

"Then, if England will, as you say, and all the world knows it, there can be no war. Germany won't be so mad as that."

On the morrow by noon we read of the German ultimatum. The day after came the declaration of war, and the Austrian mobilisation order. We were fairly caught. All that remained for me to do was to get my party out of the way of eventual shells. The best move which occurred to me was to snatch them up instantly into the mountains to a Polish health resort of great repute—which I did (at the rate of one hundred miles in eleven hours) by the last civilian train permitted to leave Cracow for the next three weeks.

And there we remained amongst the Poles from all parts of Poland, not officially interned, but simply unable to obtain the permission to travel by train, or road. It was a wonderful, a poignant two months. This is not the time, and, perhaps, not the place, to enlarge upon the tragic character of the situation; a whole people seeing the culmination of its misfortunes in a final catastrophe, unable to trust anyone, to appeal to anyone, to look for help from any quarter; deprived of all hope and even of its last illusions, and unable, in the trouble of minds and the unrest of consciences, to take refuge in stoical acceptance. I have seen all this. And I am glad I have not so many years left me to remember that appalling feeling of inexorable fate, tangible, palpable, come after so many cruel years, a figure of dread, murmuring with iron lips the final words: Ruin—and Extinction.

But enough of this. For our little band there was the awful anguish of incertitude as to the real nature of events in the West. It is difficult to give an idea how ugly and dangerous things looked to us over there. Belgium knocked down and trampled out of existence, France giving in under repeated blows, a military collapse like that of 1870, and England involved in that disastrous alliance, her army sacrificed, her people in a panic! Polish papers, of course, had no other but German sources of information. Naturally, we did not believe all we read, but it was sometimes excessively difficult to react with sufficient firmness.

We used to shut our door, and there, away from everybody, we sat weighing the news, hunting up discrepancies, scenting lies, finding reasons for hopefulness, and generally cheering each other up. But it was a beastly time. People used to come to me with very serious news and ask, "What do you think of it?" And my invariable answer was: "Whatever has happened, or is going to happen, whoever wants to make peace, you may be certain that England will not make it, not for ten years, if necessary.'"

But enough of this, too. Through the unremitting efforts of Polish friends we obtained at last the permission to travel to Vienna. Once there, the wing of the American Eagle was extended over our uneasy heads. We cannot be sufficiently grateful to the American Ambassador (who, all along, interested himself in our fate) for his exertions on our behalf, his invaluable assistance and the real friendliness of his reception in Vienna. Owing to Mr. Penfield's action we obtained the permission to leave Austria. And it was a near thing, for his Excellency has informed my American publishers since that a week later orders were issued to have us detained till the end of the war. However, we effected our hair's- breadth escape into Italy; and, reaching Genoa, took passage in a Dutch mail steamer, homeward-bound from Java with London as a port of call.

On that sea-route I might have picked up a memory at every mile if the past had not been eclipsed by the tremendous actuality. We saw the signs of it in the emptiness of the Mediterranean, the aspect of Gibraltar, the misty glimpse in the Bay of Biscay of an outward-bound convoy of transports, in the presence of British submarines in the Channel. Innumerable drifters flying the Naval flag dotted the narrow waters, and two Naval officers coming on board off the South Foreland, piloted the ship through the Downs.

The Downs! There they were, thick with the memories of my sea-life. But what were to me now the futilities of an individual past? As our ship's head swung into the estuary of the Thames, a deep, yet faint, concussion passed through the air, a shock rather than a sound, which missing my ear found its way straight into my heart. Turning instinctively to look at my boys, I happened to meet my wife's eyes. She also had felt profoundly, coming from far away across the grey distances of the sea, the faint boom of the big guns at work on the coast of Flanders—shaping the future.

FIRST NEWS—1918

Four years ago, on the first day of August, in the town of Cracow, Austrian Poland, nobody would believe that the war was coming. My apprehensions were met by the words: "We have had these scares before." This incredulity was so universal amongst people of intelligence and information, that even I, who had accustomed myself to look at the inevitable for years past, felt my conviction shaken. At that time, it must be noted, the Austrian army was already partly mobilised, and as we came through Austrian Silesia we had noticed all the bridges being guarded by soldiers.

"Austria will back down," was the opinion of all the well-informed men with whom I talked on the first of August. The session of the University was ended and the students were either all gone or going home to different parts of Poland, but the professors had not all departed yet on their respective holidays, and amongst them the tone of scepticism prevailed generally. Upon the whole there was very little inclination to talk about the possibility of a war. Nationally, the Poles felt that from their point of view there was nothing to hope from it. "Whatever happens," said a very distinguished man to me, "we may be certain that it's our skins which will pay for it as usual." A well-known literary critic and writer on economical subjects said to me: "War seems a material impossibility, precisely because it would mean the complete ruin of all material interests."

He was wrong, as we know; but those who said that Austria as usual would back down were, as a matter of fact perfectly right. Austria did back down. What these men did not foresee was the interference of Germany. And one cannot blame them very well; for who could guess that, when the balance stood even, the German sword would be thrown into the scale with nothing in the open political situation to justify that act, or rather that crime—if crime can ever be justified? For, as the same intelligent man said to me: "As it is, those people" (meaning Germans) "have very nearly the whole world in their economic grip. Their prestige is even greater than their actual strength. It can get for them practically everything they want. Then why risk it?" And there was no apparent answer to the question put in that way. I must also say that the Poles had no illusions about the strength of Russia. Those illusions were the monopoly of the Western world.

Next day the librarian of the University invited me to come and have a look at the library which I had not seen since I was fourteen years old. It was from him that I learned that the greater part of my father's MSS. was preserved there. He confessed that he had not looked them through thoroughly yet, but he told me that there was a lot of very important letters bearing on the epoch from '60 to '63, to and from many prominent Poles of that time: and he added: "There is a bundle of correspondence that will appeal to you personally. Those are letters written by your father to an intimate friend in whose papers they were found. They contain many references to yourself, though you couldn't have been more than four years old at the time. Your father seems to have been extremely interested in his son." That afternoon I went to the University, taking with me *my* eldest son. The attention of that young Englishman was mainly attracted by some relics of Copernicus in a glass case. I saw the bundle of letters and accepted the kind proposal of the librarian that he should have them copied for me during the holidays. In the range of the deserted vaulted rooms lined with books, full of august memories, and in the passionless silence of all this enshrined wisdom, we walked here and there talking of the past, the great historical past in which lived the inextinguishable spark of national life; and all around us the centuries-old buildings lay still and empty, composing themselves to rest after a year of work on the minds of another generation.

No echo of the German ultimatum to Russia penetrated that academical peace. But the news had come. When we stepped into the street out of the deserted main quadrangle, we three, I imagine, were the only people in the town who did not know of it. My boy and I parted from the librarian (who hurried home to pack up for his holiday) and walked on to the hotel, where we found my wife actually in the car waiting for us to take a run of some ten miles to the country house of an old school-friend of mine. He had been my greatest chum. In my wanderings about the world I had heard that his later career both at school and at the University had been of extraordinary brilliance—in classics, I believe. But in this, the iron-grey moustache period of his life, he informed me with badly concealed pride that he had gained world fame as the Inventor—no, Inventor is not the word—Producer, I believe would be the right term—of a wonderful kind of beetroot seed. The beet grown from this seed contained more sugar to the square inch—or was it to the square root?—than any other kind of beet. He exported this seed, not only with profit (and even to the United States), but with a certain amount of glory which seemed to have gone slightly to his head. There is a fundamental strain of agriculturalist in a Pole which no amount of brilliance, even classical, can destroy. While we were having tea outside, looking down the lovely slope of the gardens at the view of the city in the distance, the possibilities of the war faded from our minds. Suddenly my friend's wife came to us with a telegram in her hand and said calmly: "General mobilisation, do you know?" We looked at her like men aroused from a dream. "Yes," she insisted, "they are already taking the horses out of the ploughs and carts." I said: "We had better go back to town as quick as we can," and my friend assented with a troubled look: "Yes, you had better." As we passed through villages on our way back we saw mobs of horses assembled on the commons with soldiers guarding them, and groups of villagers looking on silently at the officers with their note-books checking deliveries and writing out receipts. Some old peasant women were already weeping aloud.

When our car drew up at the door of the hotel, the manager himself came to help my wife out. In the first moment I did not quite recognise him. His luxuriant black locks were gone, his head was closely cropped, and as I glanced at it he smiled and said: "I shall sleep at the barracks to- night."

I cannot reproduce the atmosphere of that night, the first night after mobilisation. The shops and the gateways of the houses were of course closed, but all through the dark hours the town hummed with voices; the echoes of distant shouts entered the open windows of our bedroom. Groups of men talking noisily walked in the middle of the roadway escorted by distressed women: men of all callings and of all classes going to report themselves at the fortress. Now and then a military car tooting furiously would whisk through the streets empty of wheeled traffic, like an intensely black shadow under the great flood of electric lights on the grey pavement.

But what produced the greatest impression on my mind was a gathering at night in the coffee-room of my hotel of a few men of mark whom I was asked to join. It was about one o'clock in the morning. The shutters were up. For some reason or other the electric light was not switched on, and the big room was lit up only by a few tall candles, just enough for us to see each other's faces by. I saw in those faces the awful desolation of men whose country, torn in three, found itself engaged in the contest with no will of its own, and not even the power to assert itself at the cost of life. All the past was gone, and there was no future, whatever happened; no road which did not seem to lead to moral annihilation. I remember one of those men addressing me after a period of mournful silence compounded of mental exhaustion and unexpressed forebodings.

"What do you think England will do? If there is a ray of hope anywhere it is only there."

I said: "I believe I know what England will do" (this was before the news of the violation of Belgian neutrality arrived), "though I won't tell you, for I am not absolutely certain. But I can tell you what I am absolutely certain of. It is this: If England comes into the war, then, no matter who may want to make peace at the end of six months at the cost of right and justice, England will keep on fighting for years if necessary. You may reckon on that."

"What, even alone?" asked somebody across the room.

I said: "Yes, even alone. But if things go so far as that England will not be alone."

I think that at that moment I must have been inspired.

WELL DONE—1918

I.

It can be safely said that for the last four years the seamen of Great Britain have done well. I mean that every kind and sort of human being classified as seaman, steward, foremast hand, fireman, lamp-trimmer, mate, master, engineer, and also all through the innumerable ratings of the Navy up to that of Admiral, has done well. I don't say marvellously well or miraculously well or wonderfully well or even very well, because these are simply over-statements of undisciplined minds. I don't deny that a man may be a marvellous being, but this is not likely to be discovered in his lifetime, and not always even after he is dead. Man's marvellousness is a hidden thing, because the secrets of his heart are not to be read by his fellows. As to a man's work, if it is done well it is the very utmost that can be said. You can do well, and you can do no more for people to see. In the Navy, where human values are thoroughly understood, the highest signal of commendation complimenting a ship (that is, a ship's company) on some achievements consists exactly of those two simple words "Well done," followed by the name of the ship. Not marvellously done, astonishingly done, wonderfully done—no, only just:

"Well done, so-and-so."

And to the men it is a matter of infinite pride that somebody should judge it proper to mention aloud, as it were, that they have done well. It is a memorable occurrence, for in the sea services you are expected professionally and as a matter of course to do well, because nothing less will do. And in sober speech no man can be expected to do more than well. The superlatives are mere signs of uninformed wonder. Thus the official signal which can express nothing but a delicate share of appreciation becomes a great honour.

Speaking now as a purely civil seaman (or, perhaps, I ought to say civilian, because politeness is not what I have in my mind) I may say that I have never expected the Merchant Service to do otherwise than well during the war. There were people who obviously did not feel the same confidence, nay, who even confidently expected to see the collapse of merchant seamen's courage. I must admit that such pronouncements did arrest my attention. In my time I have never been able to detect any faint hearts in the ships' companies with whom I have served in various capacities. But I reflected that I had left the sea in '94, twenty years before the outbreak of the war that was to apply its severe test to the quality of modern seamen. Perhaps they had deteriorated, I said unwillingly to myself. I remembered also the alarmist articles I had read about the great number of foreigners in the British Merchant Service, and I didn't know how far these lamentations were justified.

In my time the proportion of non-Britishers in the crews of the ships flying the red ensign was rather under one-third, which, as a matter of fact, was less than the proportion allowed under the very strict French navigation laws for the crews of the ships of that nation. For the strictest laws aiming at the preservation of national seamen had to recognise the difficulties of manning merchant ships all over the world. The one-third of the French law seemed to be the irreducible minimum. But the British proportion was even less. Thus it may be said that up to the date I have mentioned the crews of British merchant ships engaged in deep water voyages to Australia, to the East Indies and round the Horn were essentially British. The small proportion of foreigners which I remember were mostly Scandinavians, and my general impression remains that those men were good stuff. They appeared always able and ready to do their duty by the flag under which they served. The majority were Norwegians, whose courage and straightness of character are matters beyond doubt. I remember also a couple of Finns, both carpenters, of course, and very good craftsmen; a Swede, the most scientific sailmaker I ever met; another Swede, a steward, who really might have been called a British seaman since he had sailed out of London for over thirty years, a rather superior person; one Italian, an everlastingly smiling but a pugnacious character; one Frenchman, a most excellent sailor, tireless and indomitable under very difficult circumstances; one Hollander, whose placid manner of looking at the ship going to pieces under our feet I shall never forget, and one young, colourless, muscularly very strong German, of no particular character. Of non-European crews, lascars and Kalashes, I have had very little experience, and that was only in one steamship and for something less than a year. It was on the same occasion that I had my only sight of Chinese firemen. Sight is the exact word. One didn't speak to them. One saw them going along the decks, to and fro, characteristic figures with rolled-up pigtails, very dirty when coming off duty and very clean-faced when going on duty. They never looked at anybody, and one never had occasion to address them directly. Their appearances in the light of day were very regular, and yet somewhat ghostlike in their detachment and silence.

But of the white crews of British ships and almost exclusively British in blood and descent, the immediate predecessors of the men whose worth the nation has discovered for itself to-day, I have had a thorough experience. At first amongst them, then with them, I have shared all the conditions of their very special life. For it was very special. In my early days, starting out on a voyage was like being launched into Eternity. I say advisedly Eternity instead of Space, because of the boundless silence which swallowed up one for eighty days—for one hundred days—for even yet more days of an existence without echoes and whispers. Like Eternity itself! For one can't conceive a vocal Eternity. An enormous silence, in which there was nothing to connect one with the Universe but the incessant wheeling about of the sun and other celestial bodies, the alternation of light and shadow, eternally chasing each other over the sky. The time of the earth, though most carefully recorded by the half-hourly bells, did not count in reality.

It was a special life, and the men were a very special kind of men. By this I don't mean to say they were more complex than the generality of mankind. Neither were they very much simpler. I have already admitted that man is a marvellous creature, and no doubt those particular men were marvellous enough in their way. But in their collective capacity they can be best defined as men who lived under the command to do well, or perish utterly. I have written of them with all the truth that was in me, and with an the impartiality of which I was capable. Let me not be misunderstood in this statement. Affection can be very exacting, and can easily miss fairness on the critical side. I have looked upon them with a jealous eye, expecting perhaps even more than it was strictly fair to expect. And no wonder—since I had elected to be one of them very deliberately, very completely, without any looking back or looking elsewhere. The circumstances were such as to give me the feeling of complete identification, a very vivid comprehension that if I wasn't one of them I was nothing at all. But what was most difficult to detect was the nature of the deep impulses which these men obeyed. What spirit was it that inspired the unfailing manifestations of their simple fidelity? No outward cohesive force of compulsion or discipline was holding them together or had ever shaped their unexpressed standards. It was very mysterious. At last I came to the conclusion that it must be something in the nature of the life itself; the sea-life chosen blindly, embraced for the most part accidentally by those men who appeared but a loose agglomeration of individuals toiling for their living away from the eyes of mankind. Who can tell how a tradition comes into the world? We are children of the earth. It may be that the noblest tradition is but the offspring of material conditions, of the hard necessities besetting men's precarious lives. But once it has been born it becomes a spirit. Nothing can extinguish its force then. Clouds of greedy selfishness, the subtle dialectics of revolt or fear, may obscure it for a time, but in very truth it remains an immortal ruler invested with the power of honour and shame.

II.

The mysteriously born tradition of sea-craft commands unity in a body of workers engaged in an occupation in which men have to depend upon each other. It raises them, so to speak, above the frailties of their dead selves. I don't wish to be suspected of lack of judgment and of blind enthusiasm. I don't claim special morality or even special manliness for the men who in my time really lived at sea, and at the present time live at any rate mostly at sea. But in their qualities as well as in their defects, in their weaknesses as well as in their "virtue," there was indubitably something apart. They were never exactly of the earth earthly. They couldn't be that. Chance or desire (mostly desire) had set them apart, often in their very childhood; and what is to be remarked is that from the very nature of things this early appeal, this early desire, had to be of an imaginative kind. Thus their simple minds had a sort of sweetness. They were in a way preserved. I am not alluding here to the preserving qualities of the salt in the sea. The salt of the sea is a very good thing in its way; it preserves for instance one from catching a beastly cold while one remains wet for weeks together in the "roaring forties." But in sober unpoetical truth the sea-salt never gets much further than the seaman's skin, which in certain latitudes it takes the opportunity to encrust very thoroughly. That and nothing more. And then, what is this sea, the subject of so many apostrophes in verse and prose addressed to its greatness and its mystery by men who had never penetrated either the one or the other? The sea is uncertain, arbitrary, featureless, and violent. Except when helped by the varied majesty of the sky, there is something inane in its serenity and something stupid in its wrath, which is endless, boundless, persistent, and futile—a grey, hoary thing raging like an old ogre uncertain of its prey. Its very immensity is wearisome. At any time within the navigating centuries mankind might have addressed it with the words: "What are you, after all? Oh, yes, we know. The greatest scene of potential terror, a devouring enigma of space. Yes. But our lives have been nothing if not a continuous defiance of what you can do and what you may hold; a spiritual and material defiance carried on in our plucky cockleshells on and on beyond the successive provocations of your unreadable horizons."

Ah, but the charm of the sea! Oh, yes, charm enough. Or rather a sort of unholy fascination as of an elusive nymph whose embrace is death, and a Medusa's head whose stare is terror. That sort of charm is calculated to keep men morally in order. But as to sea-salt, with its particular bitterness like nothing else on earth, that, I am safe to say, penetrates no further than the seamen's lips. With them the inner soundness is caused by another kind of preservative of which (nobody will be surprised to hear) the main ingredient is a certain kind of love that has nothing to do with the futile smiles and the futile passions of the sea.

Being love this feeling is naturally naive and imaginative. It has also in it that strain of fantasy that is so often, nay almost invariably, to be found in the temperament of a true seaman. But I repeat that I claim no particular morality for seamen. I will admit without difficulty that I have found amongst them the usual defects of mankind, characters not quite straight, uncertain tempers, vacillating wills, capriciousness, small meannesses; all this coming out mostly on the contact with the shore; and all rather naive, peculiar, a little fantastic. I have even had a downright thief in my experience. One.

This is indeed a minute proportion, but it might have been my luck; and since I am writing in eulogy of seamen I feel irresistibly tempted to talk about this unique specimen; not indeed to offer him as an example of morality, but to bring out certain characteristics and set out a certain point of view. He was a large, strong man with a guileless countenance, not very communicative with his shipmates, but when drawn into any sort of conversation displaying a very painstaking earnestness. He was fair and candid-eyed, of a very satisfactory smartness, and, from the officer- of-the-watch point of view,—altogether dependable. Then, suddenly, he went and stole. And he didn't go away from his honourable kind to do that thing to somebody on shore; he stole right there on the spot, in proximity to his shipmates, on board his own ship, with complete disregard for old Brown, our night watchman (whose fame for trustworthiness was utterly blasted for the rest of the voyage) and in such a way as to bring the profoundest possible trouble to all the blameless souls animating that ship. He stole eleven golden sovereigns, and a gold pocket chronometer and chain. I am really in doubt whether the crime should not be entered under the category of sacrilege rather than theft. Those things belonged to the captain! There was certainly something in the nature of the violation of a sanctuary, and of a particularly impudent kind, too, because he got his plunder out of the captain's state-room while the captain was asleep there. But look, now, at the fantasy of the man! After going through the pockets of the clothes, he did not hasten to retreat. No. He went deliberately into the saloon and removed from the sideboard two big heavy, silver-plated lamps, which he carried to the fore-end of the ship and stood symmetrically on the knight-heads. This, I must explain, means that he took them away as far as possible from the place where they belonged. These were the deeds of darkness. In the morning the bo'sun came along dragging after him a hose to wash the foc'sle head, and, beholding the shiny cabin lamps, resplendent in the morning light, one on each side of the bowsprit, he was paralysed with awe. He dropped the nozzle from his nerveless hands—and such hands, too! I happened along, and he said to me in a distracted whisper: "Look at that, sir, look." "Take them back aft at once yourself," I said, very amazed, too. As we approached the quarterdeck we perceived the steward, a prey to a sort of sacred horror, holding up before us the captain's trousers.

Bronzed men with brooms and buckets in their hands stood about with open mouths. "I have found them lying in the passage outside the captain's door," the steward declared faintly. The additional statement that the captain's watch was gone from its hook by the bedside raised the painful sensation to the highest pitch. We knew then we had a thief amongst us. Our thief! Behold the solidarity of a ship's company. He couldn't be to us like any other thief. We all had to live under the shadow of his crime for days; but the police kept on investigating, and one morning a young woman appeared on board swinging a parasol, attended by two policemen, and identified the culprit. She was a barmaid of some bar near the Circular Quay, and knew really nothing of our man except that he looked like a respectable sailor. She had seen him only twice in her life. On the second occasion he begged her nicely as a great favour to take care for him of a small solidly tied-up paper parcel for a day or two. But he never came near her again. At the end of three weeks she opened it, and, of course, seeing the contents, was much alarmed, and went to the nearest police-station for advice. The police took her at once on board our ship, where all hands were mustered on the quarterdeck. She stared wildly at all our faces, pointed suddenly a finger with a shriek, "That's the man," and incontinently went off into a fit of hysterics in front of thirty-six seamen. I must say that never in my life did I see a ship's company look so frightened. Yes, in this tale of guilt, there was a curious absence of mere criminality, and a touch of that fantasy which is often a part of a seaman's character. It wasn't greed that moved him, I think. It was something much less simple: boredom, perhaps, or a bet, or the pleasure of defiance.

And now for the point of view. It was given to me by a short, black-bearded A.B. of the crew, who on sea passages washed my flannel shirts, mended my clothes and, generally, looked after my room. He was an excellent needleman and washerman, and a very good sailor. Standing in this peculiar relation to me, he considered himself privileged to open his mind on the matter one evening when he brought back to my cabin three clean and neatly folded shirts. He was profoundly pained. He said: "What a ship's company! Never seen such a crowd! Liars, cheats, thieves. . . "

It was a needlessly jaundiced view. There were in that ship's company three or four fellows who dealt in tall yarns, and I knew that on the passage out there had been a dispute over a game in the foc'sle once or twice of a rather acute kind, so that all card-playing had to be abandoned. In regard to thieves, as we know, there was only one, and he, I am convinced, came out of his reserve to perform an exploit rather than to commit a crime. But my black-bearded friend's indignation had its special morality, for he added, with a burst of passion: "And on board our ship, too—a ship like this. . ."

Therein lies the secret of the seamen's special character as a body. The ship, this ship, our ship, the ship we serve, is the moral symbol of our life. A ship has to be respected, actually and ideally; her merit, her innocence, are sacred things. Of all the creations of man she is the closest partner of his toil and courage. From every point of view it is imperative that you should do well by her. And, as always in the case of true love, all you can do for her adds only to the tale of her merits in your heart. Mute and compelling, she claims not only your fidelity, but your respect. And the supreme "Well done!" which you may earn is made over to her.

III.

It is my deep conviction, or, perhaps, I ought to say my deep feeling born from personal experience, that it is not the sea but the ships of the sea that guide and command that spirit of adventure which some say is the second nature of British men. I don't want to provoke a controversy (for intellectually I am rather a Quietist) but I venture to affirm that the main characteristic of the British men spread all over the world, is not the spirit of adventure so much as the spirit of service. I think that this could be demonstrated from the history of great voyages and the general activity of the race. That the British man has always liked his service to be adventurous rather than otherwise cannot be denied, for each British man began by being young in his time when all risk has a glamour. Afterwards, with the course of years, risk became a part of his daily work; he would have missed it from his side as one misses a loved companion.

The mere love of adventure is no saving grace. It is no grace at all. It lays a man under no obligation of faithfulness to an idea and even to his own self. Roughly speaking, an adventurer may be expected to have courage, or at any rate may be said to need it. But courage in itself is not an ideal. A successful highwayman showed courage of a sort, and pirate crews have been known to fight with courage or perhaps only with reckless desperation in the manner of cornered rats. There is nothing in the world to prevent a mere lover or pursuer of adventure from running at any moment. There is his own self, his mere taste for excitement, the prospect of some sort of gain, but there is no sort of loyalty to bind him in honour to consistent conduct. I have noticed that the majority of mere lovers of adventure are mightily careful of their skins; and the proof of it is that so many of them manage to keep it whole to an advanced age. You find them in mysterious nooks of islands and continents, mostly red-nosed and watery-eyed, and not even amusingly boastful. There is nothing more futile under the sun than a mere adventurer. He might have loved at one time—which would have been a saving grace. I mean loved adventure for itself. But if so, he was bound to lose this grace very soon. Adventure by itself is but a phantom, a dubious shape without a heart. Yes, there is nothing more futile than an adventurer; but nobody can say that the adventurous activities of the British race are stamped with the futility of a chase after mere emotions.

The successive generations that went out to sea from these Isles went out to toil desperately in adventurous conditions. A man is a worker. If he is not that he is nothing. Just nothing—like a mere adventurer. Those men understood the nature of their work, but more or less dimly, in various degrees of imperfection. The best and greatest of their leaders even had never seen it clearly, because of its magnitude and the remoteness of its end. This is the common fate of mankind, whose most positive achievements are born from dreams and visions followed loyally to an unknown destination. And it doesn't matter. For the great mass of mankind the only saving grace that is needed is steady fidelity to what is nearest to hand and heart in the short moment of each human effort. In other and in greater words, what is needed is a sense of immediate duty, and a feeling of impalpable constraint. Indeed, seamen and duty are all the time inseparable companions. It has been suggested to me that this sense of duty is not a patriotic sense or a religious sense, or even a social sense in a seaman. I don't know. It seems to me that a seaman's duty may be an unconscious compound of these three, something perhaps smaller than either, but something much more definite for the simple mind and more adapted to the humbleness of the seaman's task. It has been suggested also to me that the impalpable constraint is put upon the nature of a seaman by the Spirit of the Sea, which he serves with a dumb and dogged devotion.

Those are fine words conveying a fine idea. But this I do know, that it is very difficult to display a dogged devotion to a mere spirit, however great. In everyday life ordinary men require something much more material, effective, definite and symbolic on which to concentrate their love and their devotion. And then, what is it, this Spirit of the Sea? It is too great and too elusive to be embraced and taken to a human breast. All that a guileless or guileful seaman knows of it is its hostility, its exaction of toil as endless as its ever-renewed horizons. No. What awakens the seaman's sense of duty, what lays that impalpable constraint upon the strength of his manliness, what commands his not always dumb if always dogged devotion, is not the spirit of the sea but something that in his eyes has a body, a character, a fascination, and almost a soul—it is his ship.

There is not a day that has passed for many centuries now without the sun seeing scattered over all the seas groups of British men whose material and moral existence is conditioned by their loyalty to each other and their faithful devotion to a ship.

Each age has sent its contingent, not of sons (for the great mass of seamen have always been a childless lot) but of loyal and obscure successors taking up the modest but spiritual inheritance of a hard life and simple duties; of duties so simple that nothing ever could shake the traditional attitude born from the physical conditions of the service. It was always the ship, bound on any possible errand in the service of the nation, that has been the stage for the exercise of seamen's primitive virtues. The dimness of great distances and the obscurity of lives protected them from the nation's admiring gaze. Those scattered distant ships' companies seemed to the eyes of the earth only one degree removed (on the right side, I suppose) from the other strange monsters of the deep. If spoken of at all they were spoken of in tones of half-contemptuous indulgence. A good many years ago it was my lot to write about one of those ships' companies on a certain sea, under certain circumstances, in a book of no particular length.

That small group of men whom I tried to limn with loving care, but sparing none of their weaknesses, was characterised by a friendly reviewer as a lot of engaging ruffians. This gave me some food for thought. Was it, then, in that guise that they appeared through the mists of the sea, distant, perplexed, and simple-minded? And what on earth is an "engaging ruffian"? He must be a creature of literary imagination, I thought, for the two words don't match in my personal experience. It has happened to me to meet a few ruffians here and there, but I never found one of them "engaging." I consoled myself, however, by the reflection that the friendly reviewer must have been talking like a parrot, which so often seems to understand what it says.

Yes, in the mists of the sea, and in their remoteness from the rest of the race, the shapes of those men appeared distorted, uncouth and faint—so faint as to be almost invisible. It needed the lurid light of the engines of war to bring them out into full view, very simple, without worldly graces, organised now into a body of workers by the genius of one of themselves, who gave them a place and a voice in the social scheme; but in the main still apart in their homeless, childless generations, scattered in loyal groups over all the seas, giving faithful care to their ships and serving the nation, which, since they are seamen, can give them no reward but the supreme "Well Done."

TRADITION—1918

"Work is the law. Like iron that lying idle degenerates into a mass of useless rust, like water that in an unruffled pool sickens into a stagnant and corrupt state, so without action the spirit of men turns to a dead thing, loses its force, ceases prompting us to leave some trace of ourselves on this earth." The sense of the above lines does not belong to me. It may be found in the note-books of one of the greatest artists that ever lived, Leonardo da Vinci. It has a simplicity and a truth which no amount of subtle comment can destroy.

The Master who had meditated so deeply on the rebirth of arts and sciences, on the inward beauty of all things,—ships' lines, women's faces—and on the visible aspects of nature was profoundly right in his pronouncement on the work that is done on the earth. From the hard work of men are born the sympathetic consciousness of a common destiny, the fidelity to right practice which makes great craftsmen, the sense of right conduct which we may call honour, the devotion to our calling and the idealism which is not a misty, winged angel without eyes, but a divine figure of terrestrial aspect with a clear glance and with its feet resting firmly on the earth on which it was born.

And work will overcome all evil, except ignorance, which is the condition of humanity and, like the ambient air, fills the space between the various sorts and conditions of men, which breeds hatred, fear, and contempt between the masses of mankind, and puts on men's lips, on their innocent lips, words that are thoughtless and vain.

Thoughtless, for instance, were the words that (in all innocence, I believe) came on the lips of a prominent statesman making in the House of Commons an eulogistic reference to the British Merchant Service. In this name I include men of diverse status and origin, who live on and by the sea, by it exclusively, outside all professional pretensions and social formulas, men for whom not only their daily bread but their collective character, their personal achievement and their individual merit come from the sea. Those words of the statesman were meant kindly; but, after all, this is not a complete excuse. Rightly or wrongly, we expect from a man of national importance a larger and at the same time a more scrupulous precision of speech, for it is possible that it may go echoing down the ages. His words were:

"It is right when thinking of the Navy not to forget the men of the Merchant Service, who have shown—and it is more surprising because they have had no traditions towards it—courage as great," etc., etc.

And then he went on talking of the execution of Captain Fryatt, an event of undying memory, but less connected with the permanent, unchangeable conditions of sea service than with the wrong view German minds delight in taking of Englishmen's psychology. The enemy, he said, meant by this atrocity to frighten our sailors away from the sea.

"What has happened?" he goes on to ask. "Never at any time in peace have sailors stayed so short a time ashore or shown such a readiness to step again into a ship."

Which means, in other words, that they answered to the call. I should like to know at what time of history the English Merchant Service, the great body of merchant seamen, had failed to answer the call. Noticed or unnoticed, ignored or commanded, they have answered invariably the call to do their work, the very conditions of which made them what they are. They have always served the nation's needs through their own invariable fidelity to the demands of their special life; but with the development and complexity of material civilisation they grew less prominent to the nation's eye among all the vast schemes of national industry. Never was the need greater and the call to the services more urgent than to-day. And those inconspicuous workers on whose qualities depends so much of the national welfare have answered it without dismay, facing risk without glory, in the perfect faithfulness to that tradition which the speech of the statesman denies to them at the very moment when he thinks fit to praise their courage . . . and mention his surprise!

The hour of opportunity has struck—not for the first time—for the Merchant Service; and if I associate myself with all my heart in the admiration and the praise which is the greatest reward of brave men I must be excused from joining in any sentiment of surprise. It is perhaps because I have not been born to the inheritance of that tradition, which has yet fashioned the fundamental part of my character in my young days, that I am so consciously aware of it and venture to vindicate its existence in this outspoken manner.

Merchant seamen have always been what they are now, from their earliest days, before the Royal Navy had been fashioned out of the material they furnished for the hands of kings and statesmen. Their work has made them, as work undertaken with single-minded devotion makes men, giving to their achievements that vitality and continuity in which their souls are expressed, tempered and matured through the succeeding generations. In its simplest definition the work of merchant seamen has been to take ships entrusted to their care from port to port across the seas; and, from the highest to the lowest, to watch and labour with devotion for the safety of the property and the lives committed to their skill and fortitude through the hazards of innumerable voyages.

That was always the clear task, the single aim, the simple ideal, the only problem for an unselfish solution. The terms of it have changed with the years, its risks have worn different aspects from time to time. There are no longer any unexplored seas. Human ingenuity has devised better means to meet the dangers of natural forces. But it is always the same problem. The youngsters who were growing up at sea at the end of my service are commanding ships now. At least I have heard of some of them who do. And whatever the shape and power of their ships the character of the duty remains the same. A mine or a torpedo that strikes your ship is not so very different from a sharp, uncharted rock tearing her life out of her in another way. At a greater cost of vital energy, under the well-nigh intolerable stress of vigilance and resolution, they are doing steadily the work of their professional forefathers in the midst of multiplied dangers. They go to and fro across the oceans on their everlasting task: the same men, the same stout hearts, the same fidelity to an exacting tradition created by simple toilers who in their time knew how to live and die at sea.

Allowed to share in this work and in this tradition for something like twenty years, I am bold enough to think that perhaps I am not altogether unworthy to speak of it. It was the sphere not only of my activity but, I may safely say, also of my affections; but after such a close connection it is very difficult to avoid bringing in one's own personality. Without looking at all at the aspects of the Labour problem, I can safely affirm that I have never, never seen British seamen refuse any risk, any exertion, any effort of spirit or body up to the extremest demands of their calling. Years ago—it seems ages ago—I have seen the crew of a British ship fight the fire in the cargo for a whole sleepless week and then, with her decks blown up, I have seen them still continue the fight to save the floating shell. And at last I have seen them refuse to be taken off by a vessel standing by, and this only in order "to see the last of our ship," at the word, at the simple word, of a man who commanded them, a worthy soul indeed, but of no heroic aspect. I have seen that. I have shared their days in small boats. Hard days. Ages ago. And now let me mention a story of to-day.

I will try to relate it here mainly in the words of the chief engineer of a certain steamship which, after bunkering, left Lerwick, bound for Iceland. The weather was cold, the sea pretty rough, with a stiff head wind. All went well till next day, about 1.30 p.m., then the captain sighted a suspicious object far away to starboard. Speed was increased at once to close in with the Faroes and good lookouts were set fore and aft. Nothing further was seen of the suspicious object, but about half- past three without any warning the ship was struck amidships by a torpedo which exploded in the bunkers. None of the crew was injured by the explosion, and all hands, without exception, behaved admirably.

The chief officer with his watch managed to lower the No. 3 boat. Two other boats had been shattered by the explosion, and though another lifeboat was cleared and ready, there was no time to lower it, and "some of us jumped while others were washed overboard. Meantime the captain had been busy handing lifebelts to the men and cheering them up with words and smiles, with no thought of his own safety." The ship went down in less than four minutes. The captain was the last man on board, going down with her, and was sucked under. On coming up he was caught under an upturned boat to which five hands were clinging. "One lifeboat," says the chief engineer, "which was floating empty in the distance was cleverly manoeuvred to our assistance by the steward, who swam off to her pluckily. Our next endeavour was to release the captain, who was entangled under the boat. As it was impossible to right her, we set-to to split her side open with the boat hook, because by awful bad luck the head of the axe we had flew off at the first blow and was lost. The rescue took thirty minutes, and the extricated captain was in a pitiable condition, being badly bruised and having swallowed a lot of salt water. He was unconscious. While at that work the submarine came to the surface quite close and made a complete circle round us, the seven men that we counted on the conning tower laughing at our efforts.

"There were eighteen of us saved. I deeply regret the loss of the chief officer, a fine fellow and a kind shipmate showing splendid promise. The other men lost—one A.B., one greaser, and two firemen—were quiet, conscientious, good fellows."

With no restoratives in the boat, they endeavoured to bring the captain round by means of massage. Meantime the oars were got out in order to reach the Faroes, which were about thirty miles dead to windward, but after about nine hours' hard work they had to desist, and, putting out a sea-anchor, they took shelter under the canvas boat-cover from the cold wind and torrential rain. Says the narrator: "We were all very wet and miserable, and decided to have two biscuits all round. The effects of this and being under the shelter of the canvas warmed us up and made us feel pretty well contented. At about sunrise the captain showed signs of recovery, and by the time the sun was up he was looking a lot better, much to our relief."

After being informed of what had been done the revived captain "dropped a bombshell in our midst," by proposing to make for the Shetlands, which were *only* one hundred and fifty miles off. "The wind is in our favour," he said. "I promise to take you there. Are you all willing?" This—comments the chief engineer—"from a man who but a few hours previously had been hauled back from the grave!" The captain's confident manner inspired the men, and they all agreed. Under the best possible conditions a boat-run of one hundred and fifty miles in the North Atlantic and in winter weather would have been a feat of no mean merit, but in the circumstances it required uncommon nerve and skill to carry out such a promise. With an oar for a mast and the boat-cover cut down for a sail they started on their dangerous journey, with the boat compass and the stars for their guide. The captain's undaunted serenity buoyed them all up against despondency. He told them what point he was making for. It was Ronas Hill, "and we struck it as straight as a die."

The chief engineer commends also the ship steward for the manner in which he made the little food they had last, the cheery spirit he manifested, and the great help he was to the captain by keeping the men in good humour. That trusty man had "his hands cruelly chafed with the rowing, but it never damped his spirits."

They made Ronas Hill (as straight as a die), and the chief engineer cannot express their feelings of gratitude and relief when they set their feet on the shore. He praises the unbounded kindness of the people in Hillswick. "It seemed to us all like Paradise regained," he says, concluding his letter with the words:

"And there was our captain, just his usual self, as if nothing had happened, as if bringing the boat that hazardous journey and being the means of saving eighteen souls was to him an everyday occurrence."

Such is the chief engineer's testimony to the continuity of the old tradition of the sea, which made by the work of men has in its turn created for them their simple ideal of conduct.

CONFIDENCE—1919

I.

The seamen hold up the Edifice. They have been holding it up in the past and they will hold it up in the future, whatever this future may contain of logical development, of unforeseen new shapes, of great promises and of dangers still unknown.

It is not an unpardonable stretching of the truth to say that the British Empire rests on transportation. I am speaking now naturally of the sea, as a man who has lived on it for many years, at a time, too, when on sighting a vessel on the horizon of any of the great oceans it was perfectly safe to bet any reasonable odds on her being a British ship—with the certitude of making a pretty good thing of it at the end of the voyage.

I have tried to convey here in popular terms the strong impression remembered from my young days. The Red Ensign prevailed on the high seas to such an extent that one always experienced a slight shock on seeing some other combination of colours blow out at the peak or flag-pole of any chance encounter in deep water. In the long run the persistence of the visual fact forced upon the mind a half-unconscious sense of its inner significance. We have all heard of the well-known view that trade follows the flag. And that is not always true. There is also this truth that the flag, in normal conditions, represents commerce to the eye and understanding of the average man. This is a truth, but it is not the whole truth. In its numbers and in its unfailing ubiquity, the British Red Ensign, under which naval actions too have been fought, adventures entered upon and sacrifices offered, represented in fact something more than the prestige of a great trade.

The flutter of that piece of red bunting showered sentiment on the nations of the earth. I will not venture to say that in every case that sentiment was of a friendly nature. Of hatred, half concealed or concealed not at all, this is not the place to speak; and indeed the little I have seen of it about the world was tainted with stupidity and seemed to confess in its very violence the extreme poorness of its case. But generally it was more in the nature of envious wonder qualified by a half-concealed admiration.

That flag, which but for the Union Jack in the corner might have been adopted by the most radical of revolutions, affirmed in its numbers the stability of purpose, the continuity of effort and the greatness of Britain's opportunity pursued steadily in the order and peace of the world: that world which for twenty-five years or so after 1870 may be said to have been living in holy calm and hushed silence with only now and then a slight clink of metal, as if in some distant part of mankind's habitation some restless body had stumbled over a heap of old armour.

II.

We who have learned by now what a world-war is like may be excused for considering the disturbances of that period as insignificant brawls, mere hole-and-corner scuffles. In the world, which memory depicts as so wonderfully tranquil all over, it was the sea yet that was the safest place. And the Red Ensign, commercial, industrial, historic, pervaded the sea! Assertive only by its numbers, highly significant, and, under its character of a trade—emblem, nationally expressive, it was symbolic of old and new ideas, of conservatism and progress, of routine and enterprise, of drudgery and adventure—and of a certain easy-going optimism that would have appeared the Father of Sloth itself if it had not been so stubbornly, so everlastingly active.

The unimaginative, hard-working men, great and small, who served this flag afloat and ashore, nursed dumbly a mysterious sense of its greatness. It sheltered magnificently their vagabond labours under the sleepless eye of the sun. It held up the Edifice. But it crowned it too. This is not the extravagance of a mixed metaphor. It is the sober expression of a not very complex truth. Within that double function the national life that flag represented so well went on in safety, assured of its daily crust of bread for which we all pray and without which we would have to give up faith, hope and charity, the intellectual conquests of our minds and the sanctified strength of our labouring arms. I may permit myself to speak of it in these terms because as a matter of fact it was on that very symbol that I had founded my life and (as I have said elsewhere in a moment of outspoken gratitude) had known for many years no other roof above my head.

In those days that symbol was not particularly regarded. Superficially and definitely it represented but one of the forms of national activity rather remote from the close-knit organisations of other industries, a kind of toil not immediately under the public eye. It was of its Navy that the nation, looking out of the windows of its world-wide Edifice, was proudly aware. And that was but fair. The Navy is the armed man at the gate. An existence depending upon the sea must be guarded with a jealous, sleepless vigilance, for the sea is but a fickle friend.

It had provoked conflicts, encouraged ambitions, and had lured some nations to destruction—as we know. He—man or people—who, boasting of long years of familiarity with the sea, neglects the strength and cunning of his right hand is a fool. The pride and trust of the nation in its Navy so strangely mingled with moments of neglect, caused by a particularly thick-headed idealism, is perfectly justified. It is also very proper: for it is good for a body of men conscious of a great responsibility to feel themselves recognised, if only in that fallible, imperfect and often irritating way in which recognition is sometimes offered to the deserving.

But the Merchant Service had never to suffer from that sort of irritation. No recognition was thrust on it offensively, and, truth to say, it did not seem to concern itself unduly with the claims of its own obscure merit. It had no consciousness. It had no words. It had no time. To these busy men their work was but the ordinary labour of earning a living; their duties in their ever-recurring round had, like the sun itself, the commonness of daily things; their individual fidelity was not so much united as merely co-ordinated by an aim that shone with no spiritual lustre. They were everyday men. They were that, eminently. When the great opportunity came to them to link arms in response to a supreme call they received it with characteristic simplicity, incorporating self-sacrifice into the texture of their common task, and, as far as emotion went, framing the horror of mankind's catastrophic time within the rigid rules of their professional conscience. And who can say that they could have done better than this?

Such was their past both remote and near. It has been stubbornly consistent, and as this consistency was based upon the character of men fashioned by a very old tradition, there is no doubt that it will endure. Such changes as came into the sea life have been for the main part mechanical and affecting only the material conditions of that inbred consistency. That men don't change is a profound truth. They don't change because it is not necessary for them to change even if they could accomplish that miracle. It is enough for them to be infinitely adaptable—as the last four years have abundantly proved.

III.

Thus one may await the future without undue excitement and with unshaken confidence. Whether the hues of sunrise are angry or benign, gorgeous or sinister, we shall always have the same sky over our heads. Yet by a kindly dispensation of Providence the human faculty of astonishment will never lack food. What could be more surprising for instance, than the calm invitation to Great Britain to discard the force and protection of its Navy? It has been suggested, it has been proposed—I don't know whether it has been pressed. Probably not much. For if the excursions of audacious folly have no bounds that human eye can see, reason has the habit of never straying very far away from its throne.

It is not the first time in history that excited voices have been heard urging the warrior still panting from the fray to fling his tried weapons on the altar of peace, for they would be needed no more! And such voices have been, in undying hope or extreme weariness, listened to sometimes. But not for long. After all every sort of shouting is a transitory thing. It is the grim silence of facts that remains.

The British Merchant Service has been challenged in its supremacy before. It will be challenged again. It may be even asked menacingly in the name of some humanitarian doctrine or some empty ideal to step down voluntarily from that place which it has managed to keep for so many years. But I imagine that it will take more than words of brotherly love or brotherly anger (which, as is well known, is the worst kind of anger) to drive British seamen, armed or unarmed, from the seas. Firm in this indestructible if not easily explained conviction, I can allow myself to think placidly of that long, long future which I shall not see.

My confidence rests on the hearts of men who do not change, though they may forget many things for a time and even forget to be themselves in a moment of false enthusiasm. But of that I am not afraid. It will not be for long. I know the men. Through the kindness of the Admiralty (which, let me confess here in a white sheet, I repaid by the basest ingratitude) I was permitted during the war to renew my contact with the British seamen of the merchant service. It is to their generosity in recognising me under the shore rust of twenty-five years as one of themselves that I owe one of the deepest emotions of my life. Never for a moment did I feel among them like an idle, wandering ghost from a distant past. They talked to me seriously, openly, and with professional precision, of facts, of events, of implements, I had never heard of in my time; but the hands I grasped were like the hands of the generation which had trained my youth and is now no more. I recognised the character of their glances, the accent of their voices. Their moving tales of modern instances were presented to me with that peculiar turn of mind flavoured by the inherited humour and sagacity of the sea. I don't know what the seaman of the future will be like. He may have to live all his days with a telephone tied up to his head and bristle all over with scientific antennae like a figure in a fantastic tale. But he will always be the man revealed to us lately, immutable in his slight variations like the closed path of this planet of ours on which he must find his exact position once, at the very least, in every twenty-four hours.

The greatest desideratum of a sailor's life is to be "certain of his position." It is a source of great worry at times, but I don't think that it need be so at this time. Yet even the best position has its dangers on account of the fickleness of the elements. But I think that, left untrammelled to the individual effort of its creators and to the collective spirit of its servants, the British Merchant Service will manage to maintain its position on this restless and watery globe.

FLIGHT—1917

To begin at the end, I will say that the "landing" surprised me by a slight and very characteristically "dead" sort of shock.

I may fairly call myself an amphibious creature. A good half of my active existence has been passed in familiar contact with salt water, and I was aware, theoretically, that water is not an elastic body: but it was only then that I acquired the absolute conviction of the fact. I remember distinctly the thought flashing through my head: "By Jove! it isn't elastic!" Such is the illuminating force of a particular experience.

This landing (on the water of the North Sea) was effected in a Short biplane after one hour and twenty minutes in the air. I reckon every minute like a miser counting his hoard, for, if what I've got is mine, I am not likely now to increase the tale. That feeling is the effect of age. It strikes me as I write that, when next time I leave the surface of this globe, it won't be to soar bodily above it in the air. Quite the contrary. And I am not thinking of a submarine either. . . .

But let us drop this dismal strain and go back logically to the beginning. I must confess that I started on that flight in a state—I won't say of fury, but of a most intense irritation. I don't remember ever feeling so annoyed in my life.

It came about in this way. Two or three days before, I had been invited to lunch at an R.N.A.S. station, and was made to feel very much at home by the nicest lot of quietly interesting young men it had ever been my good fortune to meet. Then I was taken into the sheds. I walked respectfully round and round a lot of machines of all kinds, and the more I looked at them the more I felt somehow that for all the effect they produced on me they might have been so many land-vehicles of an eccentric design. So I said to Commander O., who very kindly was conducting me: "This is all very fine, but to realise what one is looking at, one must have been up."

He said at once: "I'll give you a flight to-morrow if you like."

I postulated that it should be none of those "ten minutes in the air" affairs. I wanted a real business flight. Commander O. assured me that I would get "awfully bored," but I declared that I was willing to take that risk. "Very well," he said. "Eleven o'clock to-morrow. Don't be late."

I am sorry to say I was about two minutes late, which was enough, however, for Commander O. to greet me with a shout from a great distance: "Oh! You are coming, then!"

"Of course I am coming," I yelled indignantly.

He hurried up to me. "All right. There's your machine, and here's your pilot. Come along."

A lot of officers closed round me, rushed me into a hut: two of them began to button me into the coat, two more were ramming a cap on my head, others stood around with goggles, with binoculars. . . I couldn't understand the necessity of such haste. We weren't going to chase Fritz. There was no sign of Fritz anywhere in the blue. Those dear boys did not seem to notice my age—fifty-eight, if a day—nor my infirmities—a gouty subject for years. This disregard was very flattering, and I tried to live up to it, but the pace seemed to me terrific. They galloped me across a vast expanse of open ground to the water's edge.

The machine on its carriage seemed as big as a cottage, and much more imposing. My young pilot went up like a bird. There was an idle, able- bodied ladder loafing against a shed within fifteen feet of me, but as nobody seemed to notice it, I recommended myself mentally to Heaven and started climbing after the pilot. The close view of the real fragility of that rigid structure startled me considerably, while Commander O. discomposed me still more by shouting repeatedly: "Don't put your foot there!" I didn't know where to put my foot. There was a slight crack; I heard some swear-words below me, and then with a supreme effort I rolled in and dropped into a basket-chair, absolutely winded. A small crowd of mechanics and officers were looking up at me from the ground, and while I gasped visibly I thought to myself that they would be sure to put it down to sheer nervousness. But I hadn't breath enough in my body to stick my head out and shout down to them:

"You know, it isn't that at all!"

Generally I try not to think of my age and infirmities. They are not a cheerful subject. But I was never so angry and disgusted with them as during that minute or so before the machine took the water. As to my feelings in the air, those who will read these lines will know their own, which are so much nearer the mind and the heart than any writings of an unprofessional can be. At first all my faculties were absorbed and as if neutralised by the sheer novelty of the situation. The first to emerge was the sense of security so much more perfect than in any small boat I've ever been in; the, as it were, material, stillness, and immobility (though it was a bumpy day). I very soon ceased to hear the roar of the wind and engines—unless, indeed, some cylinders missed, when I became acutely aware of that. Within the rigid spread of the powerful planes, so strangely motionless I had sometimes the illusion of sitting as if by enchantment in a block of suspended marble. Even while looking over at the aeroplane's shadow running prettily over land and sea, I had the impression of extreme slowness. I imagine that had she suddenly nose- dived out of control, I would have gone to the final smash without a single additional heartbeat. I am sure I would not have known. It is doubtless otherwise with the man in control.

But there was no dive, and I returned to earth (after an hour and twenty minutes) without having felt "bored" for a single second. I descended (by the ladder) thinking that I would never go flying again. No, never any more—lest its mysterious fascination, whose invisible wing had brushed my heart up there, should change to unavailing regret in a man too old for its glory.

SOME REFLECTIONS ON THE LOSS OF THE TITANIC—1912

It is with a certain bitterness that one must admit to oneself that the late *S.S. Titanic* had a "good press." It is perhaps because I have no great practice of daily newspapers (I have never seen so many of them together lying about my room) that the white spaces and the big lettering of the headlines have an incongruously festive air to my eyes, a disagreeable effect of a feverish exploitation of a sensational God-send. And if ever a loss at sea fell under the definition, in the terms of a bill of lading, of Act of God, this one does, in its magnitude, suddenness and severity; and in the chastening influence it should have on the self-confidence of mankind.

I say this with all the seriousness the occasion demands, though I have neither the competence nor the wish to take a theological view of this great misfortune, sending so many souls to their last account. It is but a natural *reflection*. Another one flowing also from the phraseology of bills of lading (a bill of lading is a shipping document limiting in certain of its clauses the liability of the carrier) is that the "King's Enemies" of a more or less overt sort are not altogether sorry that this fatal mishap should strike the prestige of the greatest Merchant Service of the world. I believe that not a thousand miles from these shores certain public prints have betrayed in gothic letters their satisfaction—to speak plainly—by rather ill-natured comments.

In what light one is to look at the action of the American Senate is more difficult to say. From a certain point of view the sight of the august senators of a great Power rushing to New York and beginning to bully and badger the luckless "Yamsi"—on the very quay-side so to speak—seems to furnish the Shakespearian touch of the comic to the real tragedy of the fatuous drowning of all these people who to the last moment put their trust in mere bigness, in the reckless affirmations of commercial men and mere technicians and in the irresponsible paragraphs of the newspapers booming these ships! Yes, a grim touch of comedy. One asks oneself what these men are after, with this very provincial display of authority. I beg my friends in the United States pardon for calling these zealous senators men. I don't wish to be disrespectful. They may be of the stature of demi-gods for all I know, but at that great distance from the shores of effete Europe and in the presence of so many guileless dead, their size seems diminished from this side. What are they after? What is there for them to find out? We know what had happened. The ship scraped her side against a piece of ice, and sank after floating for two hours and a half, taking a lot of people down with her. What more can they find out from the unfair badgering of the unhappy "Yamsi," or the ruffianly abuse of the same.

"Yamsi," I should explain, is a mere code address, and I use it here symbolically. I have seen commerce pretty close. I know what it is worth, and I have no particular regard for commercial magnates, but one must protest against these Bumble-like proceedings. Is it indignation at the loss of so many lives which is at work here? Well, the American railroads kill very many people during one single year, I dare say. Then why don't these dignitaries come down on the presidents of their own railroads, of which one can't say whether they are mere means of transportation or a sort of gambling game for the use of American plutocrats. Is it only an ardent and, upon the whole, praiseworthy desire for information? But the reports of the inquiry tell us that the august senators, though raising a lot of questions testifying to the complete innocence and even blankness of their minds, are unable to understand what the second officer is saying to them. We are so informed by the press from the other side. Even such a simple expression as that one of the look-out men was stationed in the "eyes of the ship" was too much for the senators of the land of graphic expression. What it must have been in the more recondite matters I won't even try to think, because I have no mind for smiles just now. They were greatly exercised about the sound of explosions heard when half the ship was under water already. Was there one? Were there two? They seemed to be smelling a rat there! Has not some charitable soul told them (what even schoolboys who read sea stories know) that when a ship sinks from a leak like this, a deck or two is always blown up; and that when a steamship goes down by the head, the boilers may, and often do break adrift with a sound which resembles the sound of an explosion? And they may, indeed, explode, for all I know. In the only case I have seen of a steamship sinking there was such a sound, but I didn't dive down after her to investigate. She was not of 45,000 tons and declared unsinkable, but the sight was impressive enough. I shall never forget the muffled, mysterious detonation, the sudden agitation of the sea round the slowly raised stern, and to this day I have in my eye the propeller, seen perfectly still in its frame against a clear evening sky.

But perhaps the second officer has explained to them by this time this and a few other little facts. Though why an officer of the British merchant service should answer the questions of any king, emperor, autocrat, or senator of any foreign power (as to an event in which a British ship alone was concerned, and which did not even take place in the territorial waters of that power) passes my understanding. The only authority he is bound to answer is the Board of Trade. But with what face the Board of Trade, which, having made the regulations for 10,000 ton ships, put its dear old bald head under its wing for ten years, took it out only to shelve an important report, and with a dreary murmur, "Unsinkable," put it back again, in the hope of not being disturbed for another ten years, with what face it will be putting questions to that man who has done his duty, as to the facts of this disaster and as to his professional conduct in it—well, I don't know! I have the greatest respect for our established authorities. I am a disciplined man, and I have a natural indulgence for the weaknesses of human institutions; but I will own that at times I have regretted their—how shall I say it?—their imponderability. A Board of Trade—what is it? A Board of . . . I believe the Speaker of the Irish Parliament is one of the members of it. A ghost. Less than that; as yet a mere memory. An office with adequate and no doubt comfortable furniture and a lot of perfectly irresponsible gentlemen who exist packed in its equable atmosphere softly, as if in a lot of cotton-wool, and with no care in the world; for there can be no care without personal responsibility—

such, for instance, as the seamen have—those seamen from whose mouths this irresponsible institution can take away the bread—as a disciplinary measure. Yes—it's all that. And what more? The name of a politician—a party man! Less than nothing; a mere void without as much as a shadow of responsibility cast into it from that light in which move the masses of men who work, who deal in things and face the realities—not the words—of this life.

Years ago I remember overhearing two genuine shellbacks of the old type commenting on a ship's officer, who, if not exactly incompetent, did not commend himself to their severe judgment of accomplished sailor-men. Said one, resuming and concluding the discussion in a funnily judicial tone:

"The Board of Trade must have been drunk when they gave him his certificate."

I confess that this notion of the Board of Trade as an entity having a brain which could be overcome by the fumes of strong liquor charmed me exceedingly. For then it would have been unlike the limited companies of which some exasperated wit has once said that they had no souls to be saved and no bodies to be kicked, and thus were free in this world and the next from all the effective sanctions of conscientious conduct. But, unfortunately, the picturesque pronouncement overheard by me was only a characteristic sally of an annoyed sailor. The Board of Trade is composed of bloodless departments. It has no limbs and no physiognomy, or else at the forthcoming inquiry it might have paid to the victims of the *Titanic* disaster the small tribute of a blush. I ask myself whether the Marine Department of the Board of Trade did really believe, when they decided to shelve the report on equipment for a time, that a ship of 45,000 tons, that *any* ship, could be made practically indestructible by means of water-tight bulkheads? It seems incredible to anybody who had ever reflected upon the properties of material, such as wood or steel. You can't, let builders say what they like, make a ship of such dimensions as strong proportionately as a much smaller one. The shocks our old whalers had to stand amongst the heavy floes in Baffin's Bay were perfectly staggering, notwithstanding the most skilful handling, and yet they lasted for years. The *Titanic*, if one may believe the last reports, has only scraped against a piece of ice which, I suspect, was not an enormously bulky and comparatively easily seen berg, but the low edge of a floe—and sank. Leisurely enough, God knows—and here the advantage of bulkheads comes in—for time is a great friend, a good helper—though in this lamentable case these bulkheads served only to prolong the agony of the passengers who could not be saved. But she sank, causing, apart from the sorrow and the pity of the loss of so many lives, a sort of surprised consternation that such a thing should have happened at all. Why? You build a 45,000 tons hotel of thin steel plates to secure the patronage of, say, a couple of thousand rich people (for if it had been for the emigrant trade alone, there would have been no such exaggeration of mere size), you decorate it in the style of the Pharaohs or in the Louis Quinze style—I don't know which—and to please the aforesaid fatuous handful of individuals, who have more money than they know what to do with, and to the applause of two continents, you launch that mass with two thousand people on board at twenty-one knots across the sea—a perfect exhibition of the modern blind trust in mere material and appliances. And then this happens. General uproar. The blind trust in material and appliances has received a terrible shock. I will say nothing of the credulity which accepts any statement which specialists, technicians and office-people are pleased to make, whether for purposes of gain or glory. You stand there astonished and hurt in your profoundest sensibilities. But what else under the circumstances could you expect?

For my part I could much sooner believe in an unsinkable ship of 3,000 tons than in one of 40,000 tons. It is one of those things that stand to reason. You can't increase the thickness of scantling and plates indefinitely. And the mere weight of this bigness is an added disadvantage. In reading the reports, the first reflection which occurs to one is that, if that luckless ship had been a couple of hundred feet shorter, she would have probably gone clear of the danger. But then, perhaps, she could not have had a swimming bath and a French cafe. That, of course, is a serious consideration. I am well aware that those responsible for her short and fatal existence ask us in desolate accents to believe that if she had hit end on she would have survived. Which, by a sort of coy implication, seems to mean that it was all the fault of the officer of the watch (he is dead now) for trying to avoid the obstacle. We shall have presently, in deference to commercial and industrial interests, a new kind of seamanship. A very new and "progressive" kind. If you see anything in the way, by no means try to avoid it; smash at it full tilt. And then—and then only you shall see the triumph of material, of clever contrivances, of the whole box of engineering tricks in fact, and cover with glory a commercial concern of the most unmitigated sort, a great Trust, and a great ship-building yard, justly famed for the super-excellence of its material and workmanship. Unsinkable! See? I told you she was unsinkable, if only handled in accordance with the new seamanship. Everything's in that. And, doubtless, the Board of Trade, if properly approached, would consent to give the needed instructions to its examiners of Masters and Mates. Behold the examination-room of the future. Enter to the grizzled examiner a young man of modest aspect: "Are you well up in modern seamanship?" "I hope so, sir." "H'm, let's see. You are at night on the bridge in charge of a 150,000 tons ship, with a motor track, organ- loft, etc., etc., with a full cargo of passengers, a full crew of 1,500 cafe waiters, two sailors and a boy, three collapsible boats as per Board of Trade regulations, and going at your three-quarter speed of, say, about forty knots. You perceive suddenly right ahead, and close to, something that looks like a large ice-floe. What would you do?" "Put the helm amidships." "Very well. Why?" "In order to hit end on." "On what grounds should you endeavour to hit end on?" "Because we are taught by our builders and masters that the heavier the smash, the smaller the damage, and because the requirements of material should be attended to."

And so on and so on. The new seamanship: when in doubt try to ram fairly—whatever's before you. Very simple. If only the *Titanic* had rammed that piece of ice (which was not a monstrous berg) fairly, every puffing paragraph would have been vindicated in the eyes of the credulous public which pays. But would it have been? Well, I doubt it. I am well aware that in the eighties the steamship Arizona, one of the "greyhounds of the ocean" in the jargon of that day, did run bows on against a very unmistakable iceberg, and managed to get into port on her collision bulkhead. But the *Arizona* was not, if I remember rightly, 5,000 tons register, let alone 45,000, and she was not going at twenty knots per hour. I can't be perfectly certain at this distance of time, but her sea-speed could not have been more than fourteen at the outside. Both these facts made for safety. And, even if she had been engined to go twenty knots, there would not have been behind that speed the enormous mass, so difficult to check in its impetus, the terrific weight of which is bound to do damage to itself or others at the slightest contact.

I assure you it is not for the vain pleasure of talking about my own poor experiences, but only to illustrate my point, that I will relate here a very unsensational little incident I witnessed now rather more than twenty years ago in Sydney, N.S.W. Ships were beginning then to grow bigger year after year, though, of course, the present dimensions were not even dreamt of. I was standing on the Circular Quay with a Sydney pilot watching a big mail steamship of one of our best-known companies being brought alongside. We admired her lines, her noble appearance, and were impressed by her size as well, though her length, I imagine, was hardly half that of the *Titanic*.

She came into the Cove (as that part of the harbour is called), of course very slowly, and at some hundred feet or so short of the quay she lost her way. That quay was then a wooden one, a fine structure of mighty piles and stringers bearing a roadway—a thing of great strength. The ship, as I have said before, stopped moving when some hundred feet from it. Then her engines were rung on slow ahead, and immediately rung off again. The propeller made just about five turns, I should say. She began to move, stealing on, so to speak, without a ripple; coming alongside with the utmost gentleness. I went on looking her over, very much interested, but the man with me, the pilot, muttered under his breath: "Too much, too much." His exercised judgment had warned him of what I did not even suspect. But I believe that neither of us was exactly prepared for what happened. There was a faint concussion of the ground under our feet, a groaning of piles, a snapping of great iron bolts, and with a sound of ripping and splintering, as when a tree is blown down by the wind, a great strong piece of wood, a baulk of squared timber, was displaced several feet as if by enchantment. I looked at my companion in amazement. "I could not have believed it," I declared. "No," he said. "You would not have thought she would have cracked an egg—eh?"

I certainly wouldn't have thought that. He shook his head, and added: "Ah! These great, big things, they want some handling."

Some months afterwards I was back in Sydney. The same pilot brought me in from sea. And I found the same steamship, or else another as like her as two peas, lying at anchor not far from us. The pilot told me she had arrived the day before, and that he was to take her alongside to-morrow. I reminded him jocularly of the damage to the quay. "Oh!" he said, "we are not allowed now to bring them in under their own steam. We are using tugs."

A very wise regulation. And this is my point—that size is to a certain extent an element of weakness. The bigger the ship, the more delicately she must be handled. Here is a contact which, in the pilot's own words, you wouldn't think could have cracked an egg; with the astonishing result of something like eighty feet of good strong wooden quay shaken loose, iron bolts snapped, a baulk of stout timber splintered. Now, suppose that quay had been of granite (as surely it is now)—or, instead of the quay, if there had been, say, a North Atlantic fog there, with a full- grown iceberg in it awaiting the gentle contact of a ship groping its way along blindfold? Something would have been hurt, but it would not have been the iceberg.

Apparently, there is a point in development when it ceases to be a true progress—in trade, in games, in the marvellous handiwork of men, and even in their demands and desires and aspirations of the moral and mental kind. There is a point when progress, to remain a real advance, must change slightly the direction of its line. But this is a wide question. What I wanted to point out here is—that the old *Arizona*, the marvel of her day, was proportionately stronger, handier, better equipped, than this triumph of modern naval architecture, the loss of which, in common parlance, will remain the sensation of this year. The clatter of the presses has been worthy of the tonnage, of the preliminary paeans of triumph round that vanished hull, of the reckless statements, and elaborate descriptions of its ornate splendour. A great babble of news (and what sort of news too, good heavens!) and eager comment has arisen around this catastrophe, though it seems to me that a less strident note would have been more becoming in the presence of so many victims left struggling on the sea, of lives miserably thrown away for nothing, or worse than nothing: for false standards of achievement, to satisfy a vulgar demand of a few moneyed people for a banal hotel luxury—the only one they can understand—and because the big ship pays, in one way or another: in money or in advertising value.

It is in more ways than one a very ugly business, and a mere scrape along the ship's side, so slight that, if reports are to be believed, it did not interrupt a card party in the gorgeously fitted (but in chaste style) smoking-room—or was it in the delightful French cafe?—is enough to bring on the exposure. All the people on board existed under a sense of false security. How false, it has been sufficiently demonstrated. And the fact which seems undoubted, that some of them actually were reluctant to enter the boats when told to do so, shows the strength of that falsehood. Incidentally, it shows also the sort of discipline on board these ships, the sort of hold kept on the passengers in the face of the unforgiving sea. These people seemed to imagine it an optional matter: whereas the order to leave the ship should be an order of the sternest character, to be obeyed unquestioningly and promptly by every one on board, with men to enforce it at once, and to carry it out methodically and swiftly. And it is no use to say it cannot be done, for it can. It has been done. The only requisite is manageableness of the ship herself and of the numbers she carries on board.

That is the great thing which makes for safety. A commander should be able to hold his ship and everything on board of her in the hollow of his hand, as it were. But with the modern foolish trust in material, and with those floating hotels, this has become impossible. A man may do his best, but he cannot succeed in a task which from greed, or more likely from sheer stupidity, has been made too great for anybody's strength.

The readers of *The English Review*, who cast a friendly eye nearly six years ago on my Reminiscences, and know how much the merchant service, ships and men, has been to me, will understand my indignation that those men of whom (speaking in no sentimental phrase, but in the very truth of feeling) I can't even now think otherwise than as brothers, have been put by their commercial employers in the impossibility to perform efficiently their plain duty; and this from motives which I shall not enumerate here, but whose intrinsic unworthiness is plainly revealed by the greatness, the miserable greatness, of that disaster. Some of them have perished. To die for commerce is hard enough, but to go under that sea we have been trained to combat, with a sense of failure in the supreme duty of one's calling is indeed a bitter fate. Thus they are gone, and the responsibility remains with the living who will have no difficulty in replacing them by others, just as good, at the same wages. It was their bitter fate. But I, who can look at some arduous years when their duty was my duty too, and their feelings were my feelings, can remember some of us who once upon a time were more fortunate.

It is of them that I would talk a little, for my own comfort partly, and also because I am sticking all the time to my subject to illustrate my point, the point of manageableness which I have raised just now. Since the memory of the lucky *Arizona* has been evoked by others than myself, and made use of by me for my own purpose, let me call up the ghost of another ship of that distant day whose less lucky destiny inculcates another lesson making for my argument. The *Douro*, a ship belonging to the Royal Mail Steam Packet Company, was rather less than one-tenth the measurement of the *Titanic*. Yet, strange as it may appear to the ineffable hotel exquisites who form the bulk of the first-class Cross- Atlantic Passengers, people of position and wealth and refinement did not consider it an intolerable hardship to travel in her, even all the way from South America; this being the service she was engaged upon. Of her speed I know nothing, but it must have been the average of the period, and the decorations of her saloons were, I dare say, quite up to the mark; but I doubt if her birth had been boastfully paragraphed all round the Press, because that was not the fashion of the time. She was not a mass of material gorgeously furnished and upholstered. She was a ship. And she was not, in the apt words of an article by Commander C. Crutchley, R.N.R., which I have just read, "run by a sort of hotel syndicate composed of the Chief Engineer, the Purser, and the Captain," as these monstrous Atlantic ferries are. She was really commanded, manned, and equipped as a ship meant to keep the sea: a ship first and last in the fullest meaning of the term, as the fact I am going to relate will show.

She was off the Spanish coast, homeward bound, and fairly full, just like the *Titanic*; and further, the proportion of her crew to her passengers, I remember quite well, was very much the same. The exact number of souls on board I have forgotten. It might have been nearly three hundred, certainly not more. The night was moonlit, but hazy, the weather fine with a heavy swell running from the westward, which means that she must have been rolling a great deal, and in that respect the conditions for her were worse than in the case of the *Titanic*. Some time either just before or just after midnight, to the best of my recollection, she was run into amidships and at right angles by a large steamer which after the blow backed out, and, herself apparently damaged, remained motionless at some distance.

My recollection is that the *Douro* remained afloat after the collision for fifteen minutes or thereabouts. It might have been twenty, but certainly something under the half-hour. In that time the boats were lowered, all the passengers put into them, and the lot shoved off. There was no time to do anything more. All the crew of the *Douro* went down with her, literally without a murmur. When she went she plunged bodily down like a stone. The only members of the ship's company who survived were the third officer, who was from the first ordered to take charge of the boats, and the seamen told off to man them, two in each. Nobody else was picked up. A quartermaster, one of the saved in the way of duty, with whom I talked a month or so afterwards, told me that they pulled up to the spot, but could neither see a head nor hear the faintest cry.

But I have forgotten. A passenger was drowned. She was a lady's maid who, frenzied with terror, refused to leave the ship. One of the boats waited near by till the chief officer, finding himself absolutely unable to tear the girl away from the rail to which she clung with a frantic grasp, ordered the boat away out of danger. My quartermaster told me that he spoke over to them in his ordinary voice, and this was the last sound heard before the ship sank.

The rest is silence. I daresay there was the usual official inquiry, but who cared for it? That sort of thing speaks for itself with no uncertain voice; though the papers, I remember, gave the event no space to speak of: no large headlines—no headlines at all. You see it was not the fashion at the time. A seaman-like piece of work, of which one cherishes the old memory at this juncture more than ever before. She was a ship commanded, manned, equipped—not a sort of marine Ritz, proclaimed unsinkable and sent adrift with its casual population upon the sea, without enough boats, without enough seamen (but with a Parisian cafe and four hundred of poor devils of waiters) to meet dangers which, let the engineers say what they like, lurk always amongst the waves; sent with a blind trust in mere material, light-heartedly, to a most miserable, most fatuous disaster.

And there are, too, many ugly developments about this tragedy. The rush of the senatorial inquiry before the poor wretches escaped from the jaws of death had time to draw breath, the vituperative abuse of a man no more guilty than others in this matter, and the suspicion of this aimless fuss being a political move to get home on the M.T. Company, into which, in common parlance, the United States Government has got its knife, I don't pretend to understand why, though with the rest of the world I am aware of the fact. Perhaps there may be an excellent and worthy reason for it; but I venture to suggest that to take advantage of so many pitiful corpses, is not pretty. And the exploiting of the mere sensation on the other side is not pretty in its wealth of heartless inventions. Neither is the welter of Marconi lies which has not been sent vibrating without some reason, for which it would be nauseous to inquire too closely. And the calumnious, baseless, gratuitous, circumstantial lie charging poor Captain Smith with desertion of his post by means of suicide is the vilest and most ugly thing of all in this outburst of journalistic enterprise, without feeling, without honour, without decency.

But all this has its moral. And that other sinking which I have related here and to the memory of which a seaman turns with relief and thankfulness has its moral too. Yes, material may fail, and men, too, may fail sometimes; but more often men, when they are given the chance, will prove themselves truer than steel, that wonderful thin steel from which the sides and the bulkheads of our modern sea-leviathans are made.

CERTAIN ASPECTS OF THE ADMIRABLE INQUIRY INTO THE LOSS OF THE TITANIC—1912

I have been taken to task by a friend of mine on the "other side" for my strictures on Senator Smith's investigation into the loss of the *Titanic*, in the number of *The English Review* for May, 1912. I will admit that the motives of the investigation may have been excellent, and probably were; my criticism bore mainly on matters of form and also on the point of efficiency. In that respect I have nothing to retract. The Senators of the Commission had absolutely no knowledge and no practice to guide them in the conduct of such an investigation; and this fact gave an air of unreality to their zealous exertions. I think that even in the United States there is some regret that this zeal of theirs was not tempered by a large dose of wisdom. It is fitting that people who rush with such ardour to the work of putting questions to men yet gasping from a narrow escape should have, I wouldn't say a tincture of technical information, but enough knowledge of the subject to direct the trend of their inquiry. The newspapers of two continents have noted the remarks of the President of the Senatorial Commission with comments which I will not reproduce here, having a scant respect for the "organs of public opinion," as they fondly believe themselves to be. The absolute value of their remarks was about as great as the value of the investigation they either mocked at or extolled. To the United States Senate I did not intend to be disrespectful. I have for that body, of which one hears mostly in connection with tariffs, as much reverence as the best of Americans. To manifest more or less would be an impertinence in a stranger. I have expressed myself with less reserve on our Board of Trade. That was done under the influence of warm feelings. We were all feeling warmly on the matter at that time. But, at any rate, our Board of Trade Inquiry, conducted by an experienced President, discovered a very interesting fact on the very second day of its sitting: the fact that the water-tight doors in the bulkheads of that wonder of naval architecture could be opened down below by any irresponsible person. Thus the famous closing apparatus on the bridge, paraded as a device of greater safety, with its attachments of warning bells, coloured lights, and all these pretty-pretties, was, in the case of this ship, little better than a technical farce.

It is amusing, if anything connected with this stupid catastrophe can be amusing, to see the secretly crestfallen attitude of technicians. They are the high priests of the modern cult of perfected material and of mechanical appliances, and would fain forbid the profane from inquiring into its mysteries. We are the masters of progress, they say, and you should remain respectfully silent. And they take refuge behind their mathematics. I have the greatest regard for mathematics as an exercise of mind. It is the only manner of thinking which approaches the Divine. But mere calculations, of which these men make so much, when unassisted by imagination and when they have gained mastery over common sense, are the most deceptive exercises of intellect. Two and two are four, and two are six. That is immutable; you may trust your soul to that; but you must be certain first of your quantities. I know how the strength of materials can be calculated away, and also the evidence of one's senses. For it is by some sort of calculation involving weights and levels that the technicians responsible for the *Titanic* persuaded themselves that a ship *not divided* by water-tight compartments could be "unsinkable." Because, you know, she was not divided. You and I, and our little boys, when we want to divide, say, a box, take care to procure a piece of wood which will reach from the bottom to the lid. We know that if it does not reach all the way up, the box will not be divided into two compartments. It will be only partly divided. The *Titanic* was only partly divided. She was just sufficiently divided to drown some poor devils like rats in a trap. It is probable that they would have perished in any case, but it is a particularly horrible fate to die boxed up like this. Yes, she was sufficiently divided for that, but not sufficiently divided to prevent the water flowing over.

Therefore to a plain man who knows something of mathematics but is not bemused by calculations, she was, from the point of view of "unsinkability," not divided at all. What would you say of people who would boast of a fireproof building, an hotel, for instance, saying, "Oh, we have it divided by fireproof bulkheads which would localise any outbreak," and if you were to discover on closer inspection that these bulkheads closed no more than two-thirds of the openings they were meant to close, leaving above an open space through which draught, smoke, and fire could rush from one end of the building to the other? And, furthermore, that those partitions, being too high to climb over, the people confined in each menaced compartment had to stay there and become asphyxiated or roasted, because no exits to the outside, say to the roof, had been provided! What would you think of the intelligence or candour of these advertising people? What would you think of them? And yet, apart from the obvious difference in the action of fire and water, the cases are essentially the same.

It would strike you and me and our little boys (who are not engineers yet) that to approach—I won't say attain—somewhere near absolute safety, the divisions to keep out water should extend from the bottom right up to the uppermost deck of *the hull*. I repeat, the *hull*, because there are above the hull the decks of the superstructures of which we need not take account. And further, as a provision of the commonest humanity, that each of these compartments should have a perfectly independent and free access to that uppermost deck: that is, into the open. Nothing less will do. Division by bulkheads that really divide, and free access to the deck from every water-tight compartment. Then the responsible man in the moment of danger and in the exercise of his judgment could close all the doors of these water-tight bulkheads by whatever clever contrivance has been invented for the purpose, without a qualm at the awful thought that he may be shutting up some of his fellow creatures in a death-trap; that he may be sacrificing the lives of men who, down there, are sticking to the posts of duty as the engine-room staffs of the Merchant Service have never failed to do. I know very well that the engineers of a ship in a moment of emergency are not quaking for their lives, but, as far as I have known them, attend calmly to their duty. We all must die; but, hang it all, a man ought to be given a chance, if not for his life, then at least to die decently. It's bad enough to have to stick down there when something disastrous is going on and any moment may be your last; but to be drowned shut up under deck is too bad. Some men of the *Titanic* died like that, it is to be feared. Compartmented, so to speak. Just think what it means! Nothing can approach the horror of that fate except being buried alive in a cave, or in a mine, or in your family vault.

So, once more: continuous bulkheads—a clear way of escape to the deck out of each water-tight compartment. Nothing less. And if specialists, the precious specialists of the sort that builds "unsinkable ships," tell you that it cannot be done, don't you believe them. It can be done, and they are quite clever enough to do it too. The objections they will raise, however disguised in the solemn mystery of technical phrases, will not be technical, but commercial. I assure you that there is not much mystery about a ship of that sort. She is a tank. She is a tank ribbed, joisted, stayed, but she is no greater mystery than a tank. The *Titanic* was a tank eight hundred feet long, fitted as an hotel, with corridors, bed-rooms, halls, and so on (not a very mysterious arrangement truly), and for the hazards of her existence I should think about as strong as a Huntley and Palmer biscuit-tin. I make this comparison because Huntley and Palmer biscuit-tins, being almost a national institution, are probably known to all my readers. Well, about that strong, and perhaps not quite so strong. Just look at the side of such a tin, and then think of a 50,000 ton ship, and try to imagine what the thickness of her plates should be to approach anywhere the relative solidity of that biscuit-tin. In my varied and adventurous career I have been thrilled by the sight of a Huntley and Palmer biscuit-tin kicked by a mule sky-high, as the saying is. It came back to earth smiling, with only a sort of dimple on one of its cheeks. A proportionately severe blow would have burst the side of the *Titanic* or any other "triumph of modern naval architecture" like brown paper—I am willing to bet.

I am not saying this by way of disparagement. There is reason in things. You can't make a 50,000 ton ship as strong as a Huntley and Palmer biscuit-tin. But there is also reason in the way one accepts facts, and I refuse to be awed by the size of a tank bigger than any other tank that ever went afloat to its doom. The people responsible for her, though disconcerted in their hearts by the exposure of that disaster, are giving themselves airs of superiority—priests of an Oracle which has failed, but still must remain the Oracle. The assumption is that they are ministers of progress. But the mere increase of size is not progress. If it were, elephantiasis, which causes a man's legs to become as large as tree-trunks, would be a sort of progress, whereas it is nothing but a very ugly disease. Yet directly this very disconcerting catastrophe happened, the servants of the silly Oracle began to cry: "It's no use! You can't resist progress. The big ship has come to stay." Well, let her stay on, then, in God's name! But she isn't a servant of progress in any sense. She is the servant of commercialism. For progress, if dealing with the problems of a material world, has some sort of moral aspect—if only, say, that of conquest, which has its distinct value since man is a conquering animal. But bigness is mere exaggeration. The men responsible for these big ships have been moved by considerations of profit to be made by the questionable means of pandering to an absurd and vulgar demand for banal luxury—the seaside hotel luxury. One even asks oneself whether there was such a demand? It is inconceivable to think that there are people who can't spend five days of their life without a suite of apartments, cafes, bands, and such-like refined delights. I suspect that the public is not so very guilty in this matter. These things were pushed on to it in the usual course of trade competition. If to-morrow you were to take all these luxuries away, the public would still travel. I don't despair of mankind. I believe that if, by some catastrophic miracle all ships of every kind were to disappear off the face of the waters, together with the means of replacing them, there would be found, before the end of the week, men (millionaires, perhaps) cheerfully putting out to sea in bath-tubs for a fresh start. We are all like that. This sort of spirit lives in mankind still uncorrupted by the so-called refinements, the ingenuity of tradesmen, who look always for something new to sell, offers to the public.

Let her stay,—I mean the big ship—since she has come to stay. I only object to the attitude of the people, who, having called her into being and having romanced (to speak politely) about her, assume a detached sort of superiority, goodness only knows why, and raise difficulties in the way of every suggestion—difficulties about boats, about bulkheads, about discipline, about davits, all sorts of difficulties. To most of them the only answer would be: "Where there's a will there's a way"—the most wise of proverbs. But some of these objections are really too stupid for anything. I shall try to give an instance of what I mean.

This Inquiry is admirably conducted. I am not alluding to the lawyers representing "various interests," who are trying to earn their fees by casting all sorts of mean aspersions on the characters of all sorts of people not a bit worse than themselves. It is honest to give value for your wages; and the "bravos" of ancient Venice who kept their stilettos in good order and never failed to deliver the stab bargained for with their employers, considered themselves an honest body of professional men, no doubt. But they don't compel my admiration, whereas the conduct of this Inquiry does. And as it is pretty certain to be attacked, I take this opportunity to deposit here my nickel of appreciation. Well, lately, there came before it witnesses responsible for the designing of the ship. One of them was asked whether it would not be advisable to make each coal-bunker of the ship a water-tight compartment by means of a suitable door.

The answer to such a question should have been, "Certainly," for it is obvious to the simplest intelligence that the more water-tight spaces you provide in a ship (consistently with having her workable) the nearer you approach safety. But instead of admitting the expediency of the suggestion, this witness at once raised an objection as to the possibility of closing tightly the door of a bunker on account of the slope of coal. This with the true expert's attitude of "My dear man, you don't know what you are talking about."

Now would you believe that the objection put forward was absolutely futile? I don't know whether the distinguished President of the Court perceived this. Very likely he did, though I don't suppose he was ever on terms of familiarity with a ship's bunker. But I have. I have been inside; and you may take it that what I say of them is correct. I don't wish to be wearisome to the benevolent reader, but I want to put his finger, so to speak, on the inanity of the objection raised by the expert. A bunker is an enclosed space for holding coals, generally located against the ship's side, and having an opening, a doorway in fact, into the stokehold. Men called trimmers go in there, and by means of implements called slices make the coal run through that opening on to the floor of the stokehold, where it is within reach of the stokers' (firemen's) shovels. This being so, you will easily understand that there is constantly a more or less thick layer of coal generally shaped in a slope lying in that doorway. And the objection of the expert was: that because of this obstruction it would be impossible to close the water-tight door, and therefore that the thing could not be done. And that objection was inane. A water-tight door in a bulkhead may be defined as a metal plate which is made to close a given opening by some mechanical means. And if there were a law of Medes and Persians that a water-tight door should always slide downwards and never otherwise, the objection would be to a great extent valid. But what is there to prevent those doors to be fitted so as to move upwards, or horizontally, or slantwise? In which case they would go through the obstructing layer of coal as easily as a knife goes through butter. Anyone may convince himself of it by experimenting with a light piece of board and a heap of stones anywhere along our roads. Probably the joint of such a door would weep a little—and there is no necessity for its being hermetically tight—but the object of converting bunkers into spaces of safety would be attained. You may take my word for it that this could be done without any great effort of ingenuity. And that is why I have qualified the expert's objection as inane.

Of course, these doors must not be operated from the bridge because of the risk of trapping the coal-trimmers inside the bunker; but on the signal of all other water-tight doors in the ship being closed (as would be done in case of a collision) they too could be closed on the order of the engineer of the watch, who would see to the safety of the trimmers. If the rent in the ship's side were within the bunker itself, that would become manifest enough without any signal, and the rush of water into the stokehold could be cut off directly the doorplate came into its place. Say a minute at the very outside. Naturally, if the blow of a right-angled collision, for instance, were heavy enough to smash through the inner bulkhead of the bunker, why, there would be then nothing to do but for the stokers and trimmers and everybody in there to clear out of the stoke-room. But that does not mean that the precaution of having water-tight doors to the bunkers is useless, superfluous, or impossible.[7]

And talking of stokeholds, firemen, and trimmers, men whose heavy labour has not a single redeeming feature; which is unhealthy, uninspiring, arduous, without the reward of personal pride in it; sheer, hard, brutalising toil, belonging neither to earth nor sea, I greet with joy the advent for marine purposes of the internal combustion engine. The disappearance of the marine boiler will be a real progress, which anybody in sympathy with his kind must welcome. Instead of the unthrifty, unruly, nondescript crowd the boilers require, a crowd of men *in* the ship but not *of* her, we shall have comparatively small crews of disciplined, intelligent workers, able to steer the ship, handle anchors, man boats, and at the same time competent to take their place at a bench as fitters and repairers; the resourceful and skilled seamen—mechanics of the future, the legitimate successors of these seamen—sailors of the past, who had their own kind of skill, hardihood, and tradition, and whose last days it has been my lot to share.

One lives and learns and hears very surprising things—things that one hardly knows how to take, whether seriously or jocularly, how to meet—with indignation or with contempt? Things said by solemn experts, by exalted directors, by glorified ticket-sellers, by officials of all sorts. I suppose that one of the uses of such an inquiry is to give such people enough rope to hang themselves with. And I hope that some of them won't neglect to do so. One of them declared two days ago that there was "nothing to learn from the catastrophe of the *Titanic*." That he had been "giving his best consideration" to certain rules for ten years, and had come to the conclusion that nothing ever happened at sea, and that rules and regulations, boats and sailors, were unnecessary; that what was really wrong with the *Titanic* was that she carried too many boats.

No; I am not joking. If you don't believe me, pray look back through the reports and you will find it all there. I don't recollect the official's name, but it ought to have been Pooh-Bah. Well, Pooh-Bah said all these things, and when asked whether he really meant it, intimated his readiness to give the subject more of "his best consideration"—for another ten years or so apparently—but he believed, oh yes! he was certain, that had there been fewer boats there would have been more people saved. Really, when reading the report of this admirably

---

[7] Since writing the above, I am told that such doors are fitted in the bunkers of more than one ship in the Atlantic trade.

conducted inquiry one isn't certain at times whether it is an Admirable Inquiry or a felicitous *opera-bouffe* of the Gilbertian type—with a rather grim subject, to be sure.

Yes, rather grim—but the comic treatment never fails. My readers will remember that in the number of *The English Review* for May, 1912, I quoted the old case of the *Arizona*, and went on from that to prophesy the coming of a new seamanship (in a spirit of irony far removed from fun) at the call of the sublime builders of unsinkable ships. I thought that, as a small boy of my acquaintance says, I was "doing a sarcasm," and regarded it as a rather wild sort of sarcasm at that. Well, I am blessed (excuse the vulgarism) if a witness has not turned up who seems to have been inspired by the same thought, and evidently longs in his heart for the advent of the new seamanship. He is an expert, of course, and I rather believe he's the same gentleman who did not see his way to fit water-tight doors to bunkers. With ludicrous earnestness he assured the Commission of his intense belief that had only the *Titanic* struck end-on she would have come into port all right. And in the whole tone of his insistent statement there was suggested the regret that the officer in charge (who is dead now, and mercifully outside the comic scope of this inquiry) was so ill-advised as to try to pass clear of the ice. Thus my sarcastic prophecy, that such a suggestion was sure to turn up, receives an unexpected fulfilment. You will see yet that in deference to the demands of "progress" the theory of the new seamanship will become established: "Whatever you see in front of you—ram it fair. . ." The new seamanship! Looks simple, doesn't it? But it will be a very exact art indeed. The proper handling of an unsinkable ship, you see, will demand that she should be made to hit the iceberg very accurately with her nose, because should you perchance scrape the bluff of the bow instead, she may, without ceasing to be as unsinkable as before, find her way to the bottom. I congratulate the future Transatlantic passengers on the new and vigorous sensations in store for them. They shall go bounding across from iceberg to iceberg at twenty-five knots with precision and safety, and a "cheerful bumpy sound"—as the immortal poem has it. It will be a teeth-loosening, exhilarating experience. The decorations will be Louis-Quinze, of course, and the cafe shall remain open all night. But what about the priceless Sevres porcelain and the Venetian glass provided for the service of Transatlantic passengers? Well, I am afraid all that will have to be replaced by silver goblets and plates. Nasty, common, cheap silver. But those who *will* go to sea must be prepared to put up with a certain amount of hardship.

And there shall be no boats. Why should there be no boats? Because Pooh-Bah has said that the fewer the boats, the more people can be saved; and therefore with no boats at all, no one need be lost. But even if there was a flaw in this argument, pray look at the other advantages the absence of boats gives you. There can't be the annoyance of having to go into them in the middle of the night, and the unpleasantness, after saving your life by the skin of your teeth, of being hauled over the coals by irreproachable members of the Bar with hints that you are no better than a cowardly scoundrel and your wife a heartless monster. Less Boats. No boats! Great should be the gratitude of passage-selling Combines to Pooh-Bah; and they ought to cherish his memory when he dies. But no fear of that. His kind never dies. All you have to do, O Combine, is to knock at the door of the Marine Department, look in, and beckon to the first man you see. That will be he, very much at your service—prepared to affirm after "ten years of my best consideration" and a bundle of statistics in hand, that: "There's no lesson to be learned, and that there is nothing to be done!"

On an earlier day there was another witness before the Court of Inquiry. A mighty official of the White Star Line. The impression of his testimony which the Report gave is of an almost scornful impatience with all this fuss and pother. Boats! Of course we have crowded our decks with them in answer to this ignorant clamour. Mere lumber! How can we handle so many boats with our davits? Your people don't know the conditions of the problem. We have given these matters our best consideration, and we have done what we thought reasonable. We have done more than our duty. We are wise, and good, and impeccable. And whoever says otherwise is either ignorant or wicked.

This is the gist of these scornful answers which disclose the psychology of commercial undertakings. It is the same psychology which fifty or so years ago, before Samuel Plimsoll uplifted his voice, sent overloaded ships to sea. "Why shouldn't we cram in as much cargo as our ships will hold? Look how few, how very few of them get lost, after all."

Men don't change. Not very much. And the only answer to be given to this manager who came out, impatient and indignant, from behind the plate- glass windows of his shop to be discovered by this inquiry, and to tell us that he, they, the whole three million (or thirty million, for all I know) capital Organisation for selling passages has considered the problem of boats—the only answer to give him is: that this is not a problem of boats at all. It is the problem of decent behaviour. If you can't carry or handle so many boats, then don't cram quite so many people on board. It is as simple as that—this problem of right feeling and right conduct, the real nature of which seems beyond the comprehension of ticket-providers. Don't sell so many tickets, my virtuous dignitary. After all, men and women (unless considered from a purely commercial point of view) are not exactly the cattle of the Western-ocean trade, that used some twenty years ago to be thrown overboard on an emergency and left to swim round and round before they sank. If you can't get more boats, then sell less tickets. Don't drown so many people on the finest, calmest night that was ever known in the North Atlantic—even if you have provided them with a little music to get drowned by. Sell less tickets! That's the solution of the problem, your Mercantile Highness.

But there would be a cry, "Oh! This requires consideration!" (Ten years of it—eh?) Well, no! This does not require consideration. This is the very first thing to do. At once. Limit the number of people by the boats you can handle. That's honesty. And then you may go on fumbling for years about these precious davits which are such a stumbling-block to your humanity. These fascinating patent davits. These davits that refuse to do three times as much work as they were meant to do. Oh! The wickedness of these davits!

One of the great discoveries of this admirable Inquiry is the fascination of the davits. All these people positively can't get away from them. They shuffle about and groan around their davits. Whereas the obvious thing to do is to eliminate the man-handled davits altogether. Don't you think that with all the mechanical contrivances, with all the generated power on board these ships, it is about time to get rid of the hundred- years-old, man-power appliances? Cranes are what is wanted; low, compact cranes with adjustable heads, one to each set of six or nine boats. And if people tell you of insuperable difficulties, if they tell you of the swing and spin of spanned boats, don't you believe them. The heads of the cranes need not be any higher than the heads of the davits. The lift required would be only a couple of inches. As to the spin, there is a way to prevent that if you have in each boat two men who know what they are about. I have taken up on board a heavy ship's boat, in the open sea (the ship rolling heavily), with a common cargo derrick. And a cargo derrick is very much like a crane; but a crane devised *ad hoc* would be infinitely easier to work. We must remember that the loss of this ship has altered the moral atmosphere. As long as the *Titanic* is remembered, an ugly rush for the boats may be feared in case of some accident. You can't hope to drill into perfect discipline a casual mob of six hundred firemen and waiters, but in a ship like the *Titanic* you can keep on a permanent trustworthy crew of one hundred intelligent seamen and mechanics who would know their stations for abandoning ship and would do the work efficiently. The boats could be lowered with sufficient dispatch. One does not want to let rip one's boats by the run all at the same time. With six boat-cranes, six boats would be simultaneously swung, filled, and got away from the side; and if any sort of order is kept, the ship could be cleared of the passengers in a quite short time. For there must be boats enough for the passengers and crew, whether you increase the number of boats or limit the number of passengers, irrespective of the size of the ship. That is the only honest course. Any other would be rather worse than putting sand in the sugar, for which a tradesman gets fined or imprisoned. Do not let us take a romantic view of the so-called progress. A company selling passages is a tradesman; though from the way these people talk and behave you would think they are benefactors of mankind in some mysterious way, engaged in some lofty and amazing enterprise.

All these boats should have a motor-engine in them. And, of course, the glorified tradesman, the mummified official, the technicians, and all these secretly disconcerted hangers-on to the enormous ticket-selling enterprise, will raise objections to it with every air of superiority. But don't believe them. Doesn't it strike you as absurd that in this age of mechanical propulsion, of generated power, the boats of such ultra- modern ships are fitted with oars and sails, implements more than three thousand years old? Old as the siege of Troy. Older! . . . And I know what I am talking about. Only six weeks ago I was on the river in an ancient, rough, ship's boat, fitted with a two-cylinder motor-engine of 7.5 h.p. Just a common ship's boat, which the man who owns her uses for taking the workmen and stevedores to and from the ships loading at the buoys off Greenhithe. She would have carried some thirty people. No doubt has carried as many daily for many months. And she can tow a twenty-five ton water barge—which is also part of that man's business.

It was a boisterous day, half a gale of wind against the flood tide. Two fellows managed her. A youngster of seventeen was cox (and a first-rate cox he was too); a fellow in a torn blue jersey, not much older, of the usual riverside type, looked after the engine. I spent an hour and a half in her, running up and down and across that reach. She handled perfectly. With eight or twelve oars out she could not have done anything like as well. These two youngsters at my request kept her stationary for ten minutes, with a touch of engine and helm now and then, within three feet of a big, ugly mooring buoy over which the water broke and the spray flew in sheets, and which would have holed her if she had bumped against it. But she kept her position, it seemed to me, to an inch, without apparently any trouble to these boys. You could not have done it with oars. And her engine did not take up the space of three men, even on the assumption that you would pack people as tight as sardines in a box.

Not the room of three people, I tell you! But no one would want to pack a boat like a sardine-box. There must be room enough to handle the oars. But in that old ship's boat, even if she had been desperately overcrowded, there was power (manageable by two riverside youngsters) to get away quickly from a ship's side (very important for your safety and to make room for other boats), the power to keep her easily head to sea, the power to move at five to seven knots towards a rescuing ship, the power to come safely alongside. And all that in an engine which did not take up the room of three people.

A poor boatman who had to scrape together painfully the few sovereigns of the price had the idea of putting that engine into his boat. But all these designers, directors, managers, constructors, and others whom we may include in the generic name of Yamsi, never thought of it for the boats of the biggest tank on earth, or rather on sea. And therefore they assume an air of impatient superiority and make objections—however sick at heart they may be. And I hope they are; at least, as much as a grocer who has sold a tin of imperfect salmon which destroyed only half a dozen people. And you know, the tinning of salmon was "progress" as much at least as the building of the *Titanic*. More, in fact. I am not attacking shipowners. I care neither more nor less for Lines, Companies, Combines, and generally for Trade arrayed in purple and fine linen than the Trade cares for me. But I am attacking foolish arrogance, which is fair game; the offensive posture of superiority by which they hide the sense of their guilt, while the echoes of the miserably hypocritical cries along the alley-ways of that ship: "Any more women? Any more women?" linger yet in our ears.

I have been expecting from one or the other of them all bearing the generic name of Yamsi, something, a sign of some sort, some sincere utterance, in the course of this Admirable Inquiry, of manly, of genuine compunction. In vain. All trade talk. Not a whisper—except for the conventional expression of regret at the beginning of the yearly report—which otherwise is a cheerful document. Dividends, you know. The shop is doing well.

And the Admirable Inquiry goes on, punctuated by idiotic laughter, by paid-for cries of indignation from under legal wigs, bringing to light the psychology of various commercial characters too stupid to know that they are giving themselves away—an admirably laborious inquiry into facts that speak, nay shout, for themselves.

I am not a soft-headed, humanitarian faddist. I have been ordered in my time to do dangerous work; I have ordered, others to do dangerous work; I have never ordered a man to do any work I was not prepared to do myself. I attach no exaggerated value to human life. But I know it has a value for which the most generous contributions to the Mansion House and "Heroes" funds cannot pay. And they cannot pay for it, because people, even of the third class (excuse my plain speaking), are not cattle. Death has its sting. If Yamsi's manager's head were forcibly held under the water of his bath for some little time, he would soon discover that it has. Some people can only learn from that sort of experience which comes home to their own dear selves.

I am not a sentimentalist; therefore it is not a great consolation to me to see all these people breveted as "Heroes" by the penny and halfpenny Press. It is no consolation at all. In extremity, in the worst extremity, the majority of people, even of common people, will behave decently. It's a fact of which only the journalists don't seem aware. Hence their enthusiasm, I suppose. But I, who am not a sentimentalist, think it would have been finer if the band of the *Titanic* had been quietly saved, instead of being drowned while playing—whatever tune they were playing, the poor devils. I would rather they had been saved to support their families than to see their families supported by the magnificent generosity of the subscribers. I am not consoled by the false, written-up, Drury Lane aspects of that event, which is neither drama, nor melodrama, nor tragedy, but the exposure of arrogant folly. There is nothing more heroic in being drowned very much against your will, off a holed, helpless, big tank in which you bought your passage, than in dying of colic caused by the imperfect salmon in the tin you bought from your grocer.

And that's the truth. The unsentimental truth stripped of the romantic garment the Press has wrapped around this most unnecessary disaster.

PROTECTION OF OCEAN LINERS[8]—1914

The loss of the *Empress of Ireland* awakens feelings somewhat different from those the sinking of the *Titanic* had called up on two continents. The grief for the lost and the sympathy for the survivors and the bereaved are the same; but there is not, and there cannot be, the same undercurrent of indignation. The good ship that is gone (I remember reading of her launch something like eight years ago) had not been ushered in with beat of drum as the chief wonder of the world of waters. The company who owned her had no agents, authorised or unauthorised, giving boastful interviews about her unsinkability to newspaper reporters ready to swallow any sort of trade statement if only sensational enough for their readers—readers as ignorant as themselves of the nature of all things outside the commonest experience of the man in the street.

No; there was nothing of that in her case. The company was content to have as fine, staunch, seaworthy a ship as the technical knowledge of that time could make her. In fact, she was as safe a ship as nine hundred and ninety-nine ships out of any thousand now afloat upon the sea. No; whatever sorrow one can feel, one does not feel indignation. This was not an accident of a very boastful marine transportation; this was a real casualty of the sea. The indignation of the New South Wales Premier flashed telegraphically to Canada is perfectly uncalled-for. That statesman, whose sympathy for poor mates and seamen is so suspect to me that I wouldn't take it at fifty per cent. discount, does not seem to know that a British Court of Marine Inquiry, ordinary or extraordinary, is not a contrivance for catching scapegoats. I, who have been seaman, mate and master for twenty years, holding my certificate under the Board of Trade, may safely say that none of us ever felt in danger of unfair treatment from a Court of Inquiry. It is a perfectly impartial tribunal which has never punished seamen for the faults of shipowners—as, indeed, it could not do even if it wanted to. And there is another thing the angry Premier of New South Wales does not know. It is this: that for a ship to float for fifteen minutes after receiving such a blow by a bare stem on her bare side is not so bad.

She took a tremendous list which made the minutes of grace vouchsafed her of not much use for the saving of lives. But for that neither her owners nor her officers are responsible. It would have been wonderful if she had not listed with such a hole in her side. Even the *Aquitania* with such an opening in her outer hull would be bound to take a list. I don't say this with the intention of disparaging this latest "triumph of marine architecture"—to use the consecrated phrase. The *Aquitania* is a magnificent ship. I believe she would bear her people unscathed through ninety-nine per cent. of all possible accidents of the sea. But suppose a collision out on the ocean involving damage as extensive as this one was, and suppose then a gale of wind coming on. Even the *Aquitania* would not be quite seaworthy, for she would not be manageable.

---

[8] The loss of the *Empress of Ireland*.

We have been accustoming ourselves to put our trust in material, technical skill, invention, and scientific contrivances to such an extent that we have come at last to believe that with these things we can overcome the immortal gods themselves. Hence when a disaster like this happens, there arises, besides the shock to our humane sentiments, a feeling of irritation, such as the hon. gentleman at the head of the New South Wales Government has discharged in a telegraphic flash upon the world.

But it is no use being angry and trying to hang a threat of penal servitude over the heads of the directors of shipping companies. You can't get the better of the immortal gods by the mere power of material contrivances. There will be neither scapegoats in this matter nor yet penal servitude for anyone. The Directors of the Canadian Pacific Railway Company did not sell "safety at sea" to the people on board the *Empress of Ireland*. They never in the slightest degree pretended to do so. What they did was to sell them a sea-passage, giving very good value for the money. Nothing more. As long as men will travel on the water, the sea-gods will take their toll. They will catch good seamen napping, or confuse their judgment by arts well known to those who go to sea, or overcome them by the sheer brutality of elemental forces. It seems to me that the resentful sea-gods never do sleep, and are never weary; wherein the seamen who are mere mortals condemned to unending vigilance are no match for them.

And yet it is right that the responsibility should be fixed. It is the fate of men that even in their contests with the immortal gods they must render an account of their conduct. Life at sea is the life in which, simple as it is, you can't afford to make mistakes.

With whom the mistake lies here, is not for me to say. I see that Sir Thomas Shaughnessy has expressed his opinion of Captain Kendall's absolute innocence. This statement, premature as it is, does him honour, for I don't suppose for a moment that the thought of the material issue involved in the verdict of the Court of Inquiry influenced him in the least. I don't suppose that he is more impressed by the writ of two million dollars nailed (or more likely pasted) to the foremast of the Norwegian than I am, who don't believe that the *Storstad* is worth two million shillings. This is merely a move of commercial law, and even the whole majesty of the British Empire (so finely invoked by the Sheriff) cannot squeeze more than a very moderate quantity of blood out of a stone. Sir Thomas, in his confident pronouncement, stands loyally by a loyal and distinguished servant of his company.

This thing has to be investigated yet, and it is not proper for me to express my opinion, though I have one, in this place and at this time. But I need not conceal my sympathy with the vehement protestations of Captain Andersen. A charge of neglect and indifference in the matter of saving lives is the cruellest blow that can be aimed at the character of a seaman worthy of the name. On the face of the facts as known up to now the charge does not seem to be true. If upwards of three hundred people have been, as stated in the last reports, saved by the *Storstad*, then that ship must have been at hand and rendering all the assistance in her power.

As to the point which must come up for the decision of the Court of Inquiry, it is as fine as a hair. The two ships saw each other plainly enough before the fog closed on them. No one can question Captain Kendall's prudence. He has been as prudent as ever he could be. There is not a shadow of doubt as to that.

But there is this question: Accepting the position of the two ships when they saw each other as correctly described in the very latest newspaper reports, it seems clear that it was the *Empress of Ireland's* duty to keep clear of the collier, and what the Court will have to decide is whether the stopping of the liner was, under the circumstances, the best way of keeping her clear of the other ship, which had the right to proceed cautiously on an unchanged course.

This, reduced to its simplest expression, is the question which the Court will have to decide.

And now, apart from all problems of manoeuvring, of rules of the road, of the judgment of the men in command, away from their possible errors and from the points the Court will have to decide, if we ask ourselves what it was that was needed to avert this disaster costing so many lives, spreading so much sorrow, and to a certain point shocking the public conscience—if we ask that question, what is the answer to be?

I hardly dare set it down. Yes; what was it that was needed, what ingenious combinations of ship-building, what transverse bulkheads, what skill, what genius—how much expense in money and trained thinking, what learned contriving, to avert that disaster?

To save that ship, all these lives, so much anguish for the dying, and so much grief for the bereaved, all that was needed in this particular case in the way of science, money, ingenuity, and seamanship was a man, and a cork-fender.

Yes; a man, a quartermaster, an able seaman that would know how to jump to an order and was not an excitable fool. In my time at sea there was no lack of men in British ships who could jump to an order and were not excitable fools. As to the so-called cork-fender, it is a sort of soft balloon made from a net of thick rope rather more than a foot in diameter. It is such a long time since I have indented for cork-fenders that I don't remember how much these things cost apiece. One of them, hung judiciously over the side at the end of its lanyard by a man who knew what he was about, might perhaps have saved from destruction the ship and upwards of a thousand lives.

Two men with a heavy rope-fender would have been better, but even the other one might have made all the difference between a very damaging accident and downright disaster. By the time the cork-fender had been squeezed between the liner's side and the bluff of the *Storstad's* bow, the effect of the latter's reversed propeller would have been produced, and the ships would have come apart with no more damage than bulged and started plates. Wasn't there lying about on that liner's bridge, fitted with all sorts of scientific contrivances, a couple of simple and effective cork-fenders—or on board of that Norwegian either? There must have been, since one ship was just out of a dock or harbour and the other just arriving. That is the time, if ever, when cork-fenders are lying about a ship's decks. And there was plenty of time to use them, and exactly in the conditions in which such fenders are effectively used. The water was as smooth as in any dock; one ship was motionless, the other just moving at what may be called dock-speed when entering, leaving, or shifting berths; and from the moment the collision was seen to be unavoidable till the actual contact a whole minute elapsed. A minute,—an age under the circumstances. And no one thought of the homely expedient of dropping a simple, unpretending rope-fender between the destructive stern and the defenceless side!

I appeal confidently to all the seamen in the still United Kingdom, from his Majesty the King (who has been really at sea) to the youngest intelligent A.B. in any ship that will dock next tide in the ports of this realm, whether there was not a chance there. I have followed the sea for more than twenty years; I have seen collisions; I have been involved in a collision myself; and I do believe that in the case under consideration this little thing would have made all that enormous difference—the difference between considerable damage and an appalling disaster.

Many letters have been written to the Press on the subject of collisions. I have seen some. They contain many suggestions, valuable and otherwise; but there is only one which hits the nail on the head. It is a letter to the *Times* from a retired Captain of the Royal Navy. It is printed in small type, but it deserved to be printed in letters of gold and crimson. The writer suggests that all steamers should be obliged by law to carry hung over their stern what we at sea call a "pudding."

This solution of the problem is as wonderful in its simplicity as the celebrated trick of Columbus's egg, and infinitely more useful to mankind. A "pudding" is a thing something like a bolster of stout rope- net stuffed with old junk, but thicker in the middle than at the ends. It can be seen on almost every tug working in our docks. It is, in fact, a fixed rope-fender always in a position where presumably it would do most good. Had the *Storstad* carried such a "pudding" proportionate to her size (say, two feet diameter in the thickest part) across her stern, and hung above the level of her hawse-pipes, there would have been an accident certainly, and some repair-work for the nearest ship-yard, but there would have been no loss of life to deplore.

It seems almost too simple to be true, but I assure you that the statement is as true as anything can be. We shall see whether the lesson will be taken to heart. We shall see. There is a Commission of learned men sitting to consider the subject of saving life at sea. They are discussing bulkheads, boats, davits, manning, navigation, but I am willing to bet that not one of them has thought of the humble "pudding." They can make what rules they like. We shall see if, with that disaster calling aloud to them, they will make the rule that every steamship should carry a permanent fender across her stern, from two to four feet in diameter in its thickest part in proportion to the size of the ship. But perhaps they may think the thing too rough and unsightly for this scientific and aesthetic age. It certainly won't look very pretty but I make bold to say it will save more lives at sea than any amount of the Marconi installations which are being forced on the shipowners on that very ground—the safety of lives at sea.

We shall see!

To the Editor of the *Daily Express*.

SIR,

As I fully expected, this morning's post brought me not a few letters on the subject of that article of mine in the *Illustrated London News*. And they are very much what I expected them to be.

I shall address my reply to Captain Littlehales, since obviously he can speak with authority, and speaks in his own name, not under a pseudonym. And also for the reason that it is no use talking to men who tell you to shut your head for a confounded fool. They are not likely to listen to you.

But if there be in Liverpool anybody not too angry to listen, I want to assure him or them that my exclamatory line, "Was there no one on board either of these ships to think of dropping a fender—etc.," was not uttered in the spirit of blame for anyone. I would not dream of blaming a seaman for doing or omitting to do anything a person sitting in a perfectly safe and unsinkable study may think of. All my sympathy goes to the two captains; much the greater share of it to Captain Kendall, who has lost his ship and whose load of responsibility was so much heavier! I may not know a great deal, but I know how anxious and perplexing are those nearly end-on approaches, so infinitely more trying to the men in charge than a frank right-angle crossing.

I may begin by reminding Captain Littlehales that I, as well as himself, have had to form my opinion, or rather my vision, of the accident, from printed statements, of which many must have been loose and inexact and none could have been minutely circumstantial. I have read the reports of the *Times* and the *Daily Telegraph*, and no others. What stands in the columns of these papers is responsible for my conclusion—or perhaps for the state of my feelings when I wrote the *Illustrated London News* article.

From these sober and unsensational reports, I derived the impression that this collision was a collision of the slowest sort. I take it, of course, that both the men in charge speak the strictest truth as to preliminary facts. We know that the *Empress of Ireland* was for a time lying motionless. And if the captain of the *Storstad* stopped his engines directly the fog came on (as he says he did), then taking into account the adverse current of the river, the *Storstad*, by the time the two ships sighted each other again, must have been barely moving *over the ground*. The "over the ground" speed is the only one that matters in this discussion. In fact, I represented her to myself as just creeping on ahead—no more. This, I contend, is an imaginative view (and we can form no other) not utterly absurd for a seaman to adopt.

So much for the imaginative view of the sad occurrence which caused me to speak of the fender, and be chided for it in unmeasured terms. Not by Captain

Littlehales, however, and I wish to reply to what he says with all possible deference. His illustration borrowed from boxing is very apt, and in a certain sense makes for my contention. Yes. A blow delivered with a boxing-glove will draw blood or knock a man out; but it would not crush in his nose flat or break his jaw for him—at least, not always. And this is exactly my point.

Twice in my sea life I have had occasion to be impressed by the preserving effect of a fender. Once I was myself the man who dropped it over. Not because I was so very clever or smart, but simply because I happened to be at hand. And I agree with Captain Littlehales that to see a steamer's stern coming at you at the rate of only two knots is a staggering experience. The thing seems to have power enough behind it to cut half through the terrestrial globe.

And perhaps Captain Littlehales is right? It may be that I am mistaken in my appreciation of circumstances and possibilities in this case—or in any such case. Perhaps what was really wanted there was an extraordinary man and an extraordinary fender. I care nothing if possibly my deep feeling has betrayed me into something which some people call absurdity.

Absurd was the word applied to the proposal for carrying "enough boats for all" on board the big liners. And my absurdity can affect no lives, break no bones—need make no one angry. Why should I care, then, as long as out of the discussion of my absurdity there will emerge the acceptance of the suggestion of Captain F. Papillon, R.N., for the universal and compulsory fitting of very heavy collision fenders on the stems of all mechanically propelled ships?

An extraordinary man we cannot always get from heaven on order, but an extraordinary fender that will do its work is well within the power of a committee of old boatswains to plan out, make, and place in position. I beg to ask, not in a provocative spirit, but simply as to a matter of fact which he is better qualified to judge than I am—Will Captain Littlehales affirm that if the *Storstad* had carried, slung securely across the stem, even nothing thicker than a single bale of wool (an ordinary, hand-pressed, Australian wool-bale), it would have made no difference?

If scientific men can invent an air cushion, a gas cushion, or even an electricity cushion (with wires or without), to fit neatly round the stems and bows of ships, then let them go to work, in God's name and produce another "marvel of science" without loss of time. For something like this has long been due—too long for the credit of that part of mankind which is not absurd, and in which I include, among others, such people as marine underwriters, for instance.

Meanwhile, turning to materials I am familiar with, I would put my trust in canvas, lots of big rope, and in large, very large quantities of old junk.

It sounds awfully primitive, but if it will mitigate the mischief in only fifty per cent. of cases, is it not well worth trying? Most collisions occur at slow speeds, and it ought to be remembered that in case of a big liner's loss, involving many lives, she is generally sunk by a ship much smaller than herself.

JOSEPH CONRAD.

A FRIENDLY PLACE

Eighteen years have passed since I last set foot in the London Sailors' Home. I was not staying there then; I had gone in to try to find a man I wanted to see. He was one of those able seamen who, in a watch, are a perfect blessing to a young officer. I could perhaps remember here and there among the shadows of my sea-life a more daring man, or a more agile man, or a man more expert in some special branch of his calling—such as wire splicing, for instance; but for all-round competence, he was unequalled. As character he was sterling stuff. His name was Anderson. He had a fine, quiet face, kindly eyes, and a voice which matched that something attractive in the whole man. Though he looked yet in the prime of life, shoulders, chest, limbs untouched by decay, and though his hair and moustache were only iron-grey, he was on board ship generally called Old Andy by his fellows. He accepted the name with some complacency.

I made my enquiry at the highly-glazed entry office. The clerk on duty opened an enormous ledger, and after running his finger down a page, informed me that Anderson had gone to sea a week before, in a ship bound round the Horn. Then, smiling at me, he added: "Old Andy. We know him well, here. What a nice fellow!"

I, who knew what a "good man," in a sailor sense, he was, assented without reserve. Heaven only knows when, if ever, he came back from that voyage, to the Sailors' Home of which he was a faithful client.

I went out glad to know he was safely at sea, but sorry not to have seen him; though, indeed, if I had, we would not have exchanged more than a score of words, perhaps. He was not a talkative man, Old Andy, whose affectionate ship-name clung to him even in that Sailors' Home, where the staff understood and liked the sailors (those men without a home) and did its duty by them with an unobtrusive tact, with a patient and humorous sense of their idiosyncrasies, to which I hasten to testify now, when the very existence of that institution is menaced after so many years of most useful work.

Walking away from it on that day eighteen years ago, I was far from thinking it was for the last time. Great changes have come since, over land and sea; and if I were to seek somebody who knew Old Andy it would be (of all people in the world) Mr. John Galsworthy. For Mr. John Galsworthy, Andy, and myself have been shipmates together in our different stations, for some forty days in the Indian Ocean in the early nineties. And, but for us two, Old Andy's very memory would be gone from this changing earth.

Yes, things have changed—the very sky, the atmosphere, the light of judgment which falls on the labours of men, either splendid or obscure. Having been asked to say a word to the public on behalf of the Sailors' Home, I felt immensely flattered—and troubled. Flattered to have been thought of in that connection; troubled to find myself in touch again with that past so deeply rooted in my heart. And the illusion of nearness is so great while I trace these lines that I feel as if I were speaking in the name of that worthy Sailor-Shade of Old Andy, whose faithfully hard life seems to my vision a thing of yesterday.

But though the past keeps firm hold on one, yet one feels with the same warmth that the men and the institutions of to-day have their merit and their claims. Others will know how to set forth before the public the merit of the Sailors' Home in the eloquent terms of hard facts and some few figures. For myself, I can only bring a personal note, give a glimpse of the human side of the good work for sailors ashore, carried on through so many decades with a perfect understanding of the end in view. I have been in touch with the Sailors' Home for sixteen years of my life, off and on; I have seen the changes in the staff and I have observed the subtle alterations in the physiognomy of that stream of sailors passing through it, in from the sea and out again to sea, between the years 1878 and 1894. I have listened to the talk on the decks of ships in all latitudes, when its name would turn up frequently, and if I had to characterise its good work in one sentence, I would say that, for seamen, the Well Street Home was a friendly place.

It was essentially just that; quietly, unobtrusively, with a regard for the independence of the men who sought its shelter ashore, and with no ulterior aims behind that effective friendliness. No small merit this. And its claim on the generosity of the public is derived from a long record of valuable public service. Since we are all agreed that the men of the merchant service are a national asset worthy of care and sympathy, the public could express this sympathy no better than by enabling the Sailors' Home, so useful in the past, to continue its friendly offices to the seamen of future generations.

Printed in the United Kingdom by
Lightning Source UK Ltd., Milton Keynes
142269UK00002B/99/P